St. Petersburg Bay Blues

by

Douglas Buchacek

If I ventured in the slipstream
Between the viaducts of your dreams
Where immobile steel rims crack
And the ditch and the backroads stop
Could you find me
Would you kiss-a my eyes
And lay me down
In silence easy
To be born again

-Van Morrison

*

A few notes about language, in ascending order of importance, and descending order of obnoxiousness:

I generally use the Library of Congress guidelines for transliterating Cyrillic into the Latin alphabet. In a few cases, I alter this in order to aid pronunciation for non-Russian speakers.

There are also several instances in the narrative when I use a Russian word in place of the English term. Sometimes the Russian word captures the meaning better, and sometimes the word just sounds cooler than the English, which is why my friends and I typically used the Russian term even when speaking in English. In a few cases, there isn't an English equivalent. I explain most of these terms in the text, but I have included a glossary at the end for reference.

Lastly, in Russian, when a voiced consonant appears at the end of a word, it is devoiced. For example, the letter "в" ("v") would be pronounced as "ф" ("f"), and "г" ("g") would be pronounced as "к" ("k"). This is why we are familiar with "Smirno*ff*" vodka, and also why . . .

*

*

"What is your name?"

"Doug."

"*Dahk?*"

"No, Doug."

"*Dook?*"

"No, Doug."

"*Duck?*"

"Douglas, my name is Douglas."

"Ah, ok, nice to meet you *Dooglas.*"

*

Поехали

Prelude: In Another World, In Another Time

I listened to *Astral Weeks* as I flew from my sister's to D.C. for Staging. I hit play as soon as we started to roll down the runway.

*

I was a Peace Corps Volunteer in Group IX of the Western Russia Program from August 2001 until February 2003. Our training site was in Zelenograd, an administrative *okrug* of Moscow. It was basically a suburb. In late October, I went out to site in Vladimir, where I lived until August 2002. From there, I moved to Ekaterinburg, where I remained until February 2003. Apart from these postings, I traveled extensively around Russia, spending time in St. Petersburg - where I had studied while in college - Moscow, Murom, Uglich, Nizhny Novgorod, Irkutsk, and Lake Baikal, to say nothing of smaller locales in and around Vladimirskaya and Sverdlovskaya Oblasts. I took a trip in the summer of 2002 to Prague, and went to the Baltics a couple of times. Everywhere I went, I carried a composition book, which I titled "St. Petersburg Bay Blues." In it I wrote songs, poems, and the odd note or observation. This was how I interpreted and processed my life in Russia.

This notebook was taken from my house in 2015 in a burglary.

Fortunately, if manuscripts don't burn, then they can't be stolen. While the book, as well as the photographs and postcards I folded into its pages, are gone forever, many of the words remained in my head, as do my recollections of writing them.

*

I've been trying since I came home to properly document my time in Russia. In the first year I was back, I dumped a lot of raw memories into a document. I wasn't writing with any sense of direction or structure. It was part of the process of coming home, like putting photos in an album, which of course I did too. I'm glad I did it, but reading it now, it comes off as callow and pretentious. I had obviously not gotten over or come to terms with what had happened or how it ended. Moreover, I didn't know what to write. It's an incoherent collection of memories, spliced with ham-handed history and juvenile political commentary. Still, there's a utility in it, a level of detail that I wouldn't otherwise have. At its best, it describes the mundane particulars of my day to day: the contents of the room I lived in, the approximate time it took to walk from one part of town to another, a lazy Saturday afternoon that may not have been special in any particular way but seemed evocative when I was writing the first draft of the story. I occasionally dropped the pose I had adopted and produced something almost journalistic, a record of what I had just been through.

I made another attempt a decade later, jotting down specific moments I remembered, visceral memories, tiny episodes - *interludes* - that maybe added up to more of a holistic story. Although written many years later, these were memories that were still vivid to me, and I took that to mean a level of importance - no matter how trivial, I obviously still remembered them for a reason.

When I lost the original text of St. Petersburg Bay Blues, I scrambled to write what I could remember, thinking that I hadn't devoted much mental space to these words for the very reason that I had written them down. I didn't want to lose these musings.

The songs were easy - matched to chords and melodies, I'll always remember those. But the poems and lyrics I didn't bother setting to music, and songs I didn't play anymore - that seemed more critical. I did what I could, though of course I couldn't possibly be complete. I eventually decided that those songs and the like, whether complete or not, could form a basis of a remembrance of my time in Russia, that I could use them as a jumping off point to finally sketch out such an extraordinary period of my life.

That's what I have here, my attempt to document an experience that seems simultaneously alien and essential to my life. I'm using songs and poems as the starting point, but I recognize the limitations of that approach. I wrote about a subset of my experience, and certainly didn't touch on everything. I supplement these with new essays and stories, informed by my earlier writing, as well as other sources: photographs, letters, conversations with friends, the complete volume of emails I sent to my mother while in Peace Corps, which, missing her calling as an archivist, she printed and saved for me.

It's more or less chronological, but not always. I'm not trying to say anything in particular about what I was or wasn't doing, about the context in which I was doing it, or trying to figure out what it all means. I'm trying to write about as many facets of my life as I can, but I'm not going to be a completist and in all honesty, a lot of my life there was rather uninteresting. The best frame I can put around it is actually one from my original attempt at writing about Russia, in 2003. I prefaced the text by quoting Michael Herr's *Dispatches*. He writes:

> You wondered whether, in time, it would all slip away and become like everything else distant, but you doubted it, and for good reason. The friendships lasted, some even deepened, but our gatherings were always stalked by longing and emptiness, more than a touch of Legion Post Night. Smoking dope, listening to the Mothers and Jimi Hendrix, remembering compulsively, telling war stories. But then, there's nothing wrong with that. War stories aren't really anything more than stories about people anyway.

I obviously wasn't at war and I guess I'm worried that it *will* slip away. But I'll take that last sentiment. If nothing else, these are stories about people.

***

Concrete Jungle

There's a classic Soviet film called *The Irony of Fate*. The plot is set in motion when a group of friends get drunk on New Year's Eve and one of them is accidentally and unknowingly put on a plane flying from Moscow, where he lives, to Leningrad, where he doesn't live. When he arrives, still drunk and unaware of where he is, he stumbles into a taxi and asks to be taken to his home address on 3rd Builder's Street, a quintessentially Soviet street name that isn't any more poetic in Russian. Since there is also a 3rd Builder's Street in Leningrad, as there is in every town, the taxi driver obliges. The hero emerges from the taxi, sees a concrete apartment block identical to the one he lives in in Moscow, and ascends the elevator to "his" floor. His key of course fits into the lock, since it's the same mass-produced key to the same mass-produced lock in the same mass-produced door of an apartment in a mass-produced prefab tower block. He opens the door. Even the furniture is the same. He goes inside.

Hilarity ensues.

It's a funny movie, part love story, part wry commentary on the drabness of the Brezhnev era. You could write a similar story taking place in the little boxes made of ticky-tacky on the hillsides of American suburbia.

Or in Zelenograd.

Zelenograd, the Moscow suburb where we lived for two months during Training, was one of these places, a faceless nowhere that could be anywhere. Though lots of

Russian cities were ringed by such a sea of concrete, at least there was usually a historic core. Not in Zelenograd. It was a planned city built almost entirely in the 1960s and '70s. Even if there had been an Old Town Zelenograd at one point, it would've been obliterated during the war, as the Fascists made it to the future Zelenograd - but no further - during the Battle of Moscow.

I've struggled with what to write about Zelenograd, but perhaps that inability to say anything substantive about it is fitting. There wasn't much to the town. My time there is a blur. We found out our sites fairly soon after arrival and at that point my mental energy was decidedly not in Zelenograd. I guess if the point of *The Irony of Fate* is that there is real emotional warmth inside those cold apartment blocks, it makes sense that episodes involving people are the primary takeaways of my time in Zelenograd, and that all of the photographs I took in the city were taken inside.

Many of my memories involve crowding around the tiny table in Larissa's kitchen, drinking beer, as she sang Soviet folk songs on guitar. Larissa was my friend Laura's host mom. She was an exuberant Armenian. "Podmoskovnye Vechera" was her go-to, from which she would transition to "Hotel California," an oddball medley if there ever was one. She opened her tiny apartment to as many Volunteers as could fit in her kitchen. It became our clubhouse.

Though most of our time there was joyful, she also gave us a place to gather on the evening of September 11th, to be together, in shock, worried, as she poured us screwdrivers to numb the grief. Laura called to invite me over that night, and as I was about to hang up the phone and head out, I heard Laura yelling through the receiver.

"What is it?"

"Larissa says to get her some cigarettes on the way."

"Ok."

"And vodka."

"Ok."

I never knew if it was Larissa asking for that, or Laura.

*

Interlude: We Are the Skyscraper Condemnation Affiliate

I remember standing on a pile of rubble near my apartment in Zelenograd, smoking cigarettes, and talking to John Anderson one day in the fall of 2001. For some reason, there was a pile of rubble, and this was completely normal.

*

We were the ninth group of Peace Corps Volunteers in Western Russia since the Program opened in 1992. There was another group of Volunteers in Russia, based in Vladivostok in the Far East, but they may as well have been on another planet. The Volunteers in our group were from all over the United States, which is pretty much where our diversity ended. Most of us were young, recently out of college, or just a couple of years removed, although we did have a few retirees in the group, and some who were near that impossible age of thirty. It didn't take long for us to bond. Connecting was easy - if nothing else we could fall back on the strange brew of culture shock, nerves, and excitement all of us were feeling. We had each other in common, which was more than enough to bridge any gap in our own personal interests when conversations stalled.

I felt this connection from the beginning. When I arrived in D.C. for Staging, my college friend Tracy picked me up at the airport. We had lunch together, and then she dropped me off at a hotel on Dupont Circle. I took a deep breath and walked into the lobby. Standing by the front desk was a guy about my age, a tangle of curly hair perched on top of his head, long sideburns crawling down his cheeks. "He's got to be one of us," I thought to myself. He was. I eventually learned that he was Dave, but we started calling him "Pushkin" once we got to Russia. Dave was my first encounter with "us," and it was as if I was checking into our group when I got to the counter and told them my name. A few months before, Peace Corps had sent out a mailing with lots of information about what was to come. It included a roster of our group, fifty-five names that meant nothing to me. Dave's was one of them. Now here he was, the first to become more than theoretical, checking into the hotel at the same time as I was. It was the first step of creating "us."

In addition to Dave, "us" soon came to include my roommate for the night – oddly enough, one of the few Volunteers I came to actively dislike – and a conference room filled with several dozen temporary strangers. Right away, I felt pretty at ease with just about all of my new comrades, though we eventually divided ourselves into smaller subgroups, to make a cohort of fifty-six more manageable. By the end of that first day, I had already assembled the beginnings of a group that would become some of the deepest friends I've made in my life.

I met Laura in the hotel in D.C., and we hit it off right away. It's probably fair to say that Laura was my first friend in Peace Corps. As I sat at a table, alone, at the hotel bar, nervously sipping a beer, she came over and asked to sit down. Of course. I remember we talked about *The Simpsons*. I liked Laura from the start. Although I was certainly attracted to Laura, and loved being around her, my feelings about Laura were (and are) relatively simple. She's one of my favorite people in any and all contexts, and even when our relationship became physical at various times, it didn't complicate matters. Everything that happened between us was a natural extension of being pals, and I've always loved the purity of that.

I remember meeting Adam during one of the ice breaker activities, also on the first day. He had advanced scouting on me - coincidentally, I had studied in St. Petersburg with several people he had gone to college with at Georgetown. They knew we were going to be in the same group and told him we'd probably get along. They were right.

Mutual friends or no, Adam and I were friends from the start. He didn't go out with any of us that first night we were together in D.C., but I connected with him at some point by the time we got to Dulles the next day. I remember driving by the Mall after we departed the hotel, an image of America in panorama as we began our journey away from it. At Dulles, Adam and I ate McDonald's and talked about indie rock before our flight, a suitably incongruous beginning to the most incongruous period of my life.

My memories of meeting my other close friends are murkier. I don't have strong recollections of Melanie before we found out we were both going to Vladimir, but few people ended up meaning as much to me. I don't know how I could have managed that first year without Melanie. She was the perfect person to spend that period of my life with. She had an intellect I looked up to, a righteousness which kept me in check and shaped my own views of the world, and a wicked wit tempered by a sweet vulnerability. I felt like her kid brother, like I had to impress her or prove myself to her. I remember once she corrected my mispronunciation of the word "detritus," when the only reason I had chosen to even utter that word in the first place was that I thought she'd think I was smart for using it. She pushed me to be a better person. If there's such a thing as a platonic soul mate, that's what Melanie was for me while we were in Vladimir (and for a long time beyond).

I'm not sure how exactly I met Simon but my earliest memory was the very first night in D.C. going with him and a big group of Volunteers to a Mexican restaurant for dinner. It's entered into legend that Simon, a D.C. native, got us lost on the way back to the hotel, but I don't really remember that. I don't know if Simon and I even spoke on that outing, but by the first week or two in Zelenograd we were friends. Simon is someone else, like Melanie, I looked up to. I often felt like a bit of a pretentious brat trying to impress Simon, but I was always knocked out by his thoughtful intellect and his self-deprecating, nervous manner. It was an attractive combination. Simon was generous with comments about the songs I wrote and it always thrilled me when he liked something I did. And I still smile thinking about the toothy grin he flashes while laughing, which is frequent.

I vaguely remember being introduced to Chris fairly early on in Zelenograd. I have no idea who introduced us, but they knew we were both from Chapel Hill. It's hard for me to think about Chris in a Peace Corps context now, as we have continued to live close to each other and we see each other all the time. Peace Corps and Russia is a tiny fraction of our friendship, no matter how foundational it is, and it's sometimes odd when it comes up during the course of our conversations, as if he's an emissary from a previous existence. I remember thinking, in the months before going, those thoughts you have when you're young, about who is "out there somewhere." I distinctly remember wondering if there was someone "out there" preparing to go to the Peace Corps in Russia who would become my best friend. There was, and what's amazing is that Chris was only a couple of miles away, if that, from me at the time that I wondered that. We both had to travel all the way from Chapel Hill to Russia to find each other.

Laura, Adam Melanie, Simon, Chris - they were my core. There were lots of others too of course. Andrew and Rob were great friends even if I wasn't as close to them as the others. Our whole cohort was pretty tight as I recall. I can think of any number of anecdotes involving just about every single person in our group - John Anderson loudly playing "Back in the USSR" on his Walkman speakers as we were stuck in traffic on the way to Zelenograd after we landed in Moscow. John Anderson had previously been a Peace Corps Volunteer in Uzbekistan, and had been planning this particular musical interlude for months. Or Micah and I organizing a home run derby on the shores of Lake Baikal after carving a bat out of a tree branch. Or Dave standing by the front desk at the hotel, looking cool, like Pushkin. There were a lot of good people and I'm grateful to have shared this episode of life with them.

*

Our training sessions in Zelenograd were at a local institute, the Moscow Institute of Business Administration. It was close enough to where I lived for me to amble my way there by cutting across the stretch of train tracks and a wedge of undeveloped no-man's land that divided my section of town from the rest, but I usually took the long way around, walking through the *rynok* before catching a bus that led up Panfilovsky Prospekt. Sometimes I'd just walk the whole way. I didn't really live near anybody, so my commute was a rare bit of alone time, which I enjoyed. I was so happy to be back in Russia. The mellifluous chatter of the *babushki* in the *rynok*, the loping Cyrillic scrawled on the chalkboard placards, even the omnipresent diesel fumes spat out by the *marshrutki* triggered fond memories of my semester in St. Petersburg, just two years in the past.

There was a lake not far from the Institute. After class, my friends and I would buy beers from the kiosk across the street from the school, follow the pathway through the woods, and hang out down by the water until it was time to stumble back to our respective microregions. On weekends we would go into Moscow. Some of the Volunteers stayed in the city late into the night or morning, sampling the vaunted and wild nightlife of a city that was pretty decadent and freewheeling at the time, but my friends and I mostly played tourist, catching a bus into town first thing in the morning on a Saturday and leaving in the early evening, having wandered around Red Square, or Patriarch's Pond, or Novodevichy Cemetery, or Gorky Park.

Given where we were, what was happening back home, and what we were about to do, we were remarkably carefree.

*

Part of the reason I was so carefree was the ebullient sense of excitement and happiness I had at being back in Russia. I was where I wanted to be. Moving to Russia as a Peace Corps Volunteer was the culmination of an obsession with the place I had developed towards the end of my undergraduate studies, though its roots stretched back even further.

For reasons that remain a mystery to me, the Social Studies teachers in the seventh and eighth grades at my middle school in Wilmington, Delaware were Russophiles. In the seventh grade, we learned rudimentary Russian vocabulary and how to read Cyrillic. The following year, I was lucky enough to participate in the annual eighth grade school trip to the Soviet Union, which the history teacher had been leading for over a decade at the time.

This was a journey over what remained of the Iron Curtain. The dénouement of the Cold War was the first news story I remember following with interest. I stayed up late to stare at the TV, mesmerized, watching the Berlin Wall being dismantled when I was in the seventh grade. While perhaps a bit too young to really appreciate the seriousness of the superpower competition - I don't recall being traumatized by *The Day After* – I had an intuitive sense of the gravity of what I was witnessing, and a belief that the world in which I was going to grow up was going to be different than before, and better, almost by definition.

From enemies to friends.

After my trip to the Soviet Union, I had a Soviet pen pal, and we traded letters back and forth, writing about the music we liked, and what we did with our friends, all of which was cut with superficial commentary about how amazing it was that our countries were on good terms. I remember him writing to me that he thought it was a good thing that his city was now called "St. Petersburg" instead of "Leningrad," and that his country was "Russia," not "the Soviet Union." That we were even writing to each other seemed profound to me at the age of fourteen. I didn't know what personal diplomacy was, but I was intuitively into it. This stayed with me.

When I began college four years later, I started studying Russian. I was not a natural. I stuck with it for four years, in part due to my own preference for stasis, but mostly due to the close-knit community. I had lost some of the callow idealism that fueled my earlier curiosity, and had also developed a lot of other interests, but the Russian program was small, and it helped to shrink down a giant university into something more manageable. Still, Russian existed as a parallel world to my "normal" university life. I majored in history, but didn't take a single Russian history class, and I never had the thought to. My focus, such as it was, was elsewhere. I was interested in American history and to the extent that I had interest in pursuing a degree beyond the undergraduate level, it was geared towards that. Russian was a separate world; it was just a fun hobby that sounded impressive when I told people about it.

Despite this, Russian was always there, even if in the background. During my senior year, I decided to stay enrolled for an extra semester in order to participate in a study abroad program in St. Petersburg during the fall of 1999. I didn't quite know what to expect, but at the very least it seemed like a fun way to put off adult responsibilities that came with graduation. I'd go overseas for a bit, come back, and start my life for real.

The four months I spent in St. Petersburg were revelatory. What began as a diversionary lark became a course correction for my life. I was fascinated by everything. The language that I had treated as an afterthought in college became a puzzle I had to solve. The history I had so blithely ignored during my undergraduate studies became an inexhaustible source of fascination. I may have not figured out what I was going to do with my life, but I had a newfound direction. I knew there was more that I had to learn. And I knew I wanted to go back.

Over the next eighteen months, I investigated a number of programs to go back to Russia, but I kept returning to the idea of the Peace Corps. I had always admired the mission of the agency. They had a program in Russia. Their mission was primarily focused on teaching English, which I figured I could stumble my way through. It would be free. And it would last two years, long enough for an immersive experience, as well as to buy me some time to figure out my life. It seemed perfect.

But I'd have to do a bit of finagling. At the time, potential Volunteers weren't given the opportunity to choose their site. There was a question on the application that asked if there was a particular place you wanted to be posted, along with a space to explain why. I wrote "Russia" and hoped for the best. During my interview, the recruiter asked about my response. I told him that I had Russian language experience, and that I wanted to improve it, and figured knowing the language would help as I taught English. He said if Russian language was what I wanted, he could nominate me into the Central Asia Program. "You'll wind up in one of the '-stans.' Or I could nominate you into Eastern Europe. You might get Russia. But you might get Hungary."

It was worth the risk, and it ultimately paid off. In July 2001, I received word I would join Group IX of the Western Russia Program. I'd fly to D.C. in August for Staging, before traveling to Zelenograd. A follow-up letter said that "[t]raining promises to be intense, demanding, at times difficult and frustrating, and fun." That was fine by me. I was going back to Russia. That's all that mattered.

*

Interlude: The Clay Machine Gun

I remember dropping into several bookshops in Zelenograd on my way home on a Tuesday afternoon in mid-September, looking for a copy of a Viktor Pelevin book in Russian. The deep blue sky that day was identical to the one across the world in New York.

*

As advertised, our training sessions were intense and demanding and difficult and frustrating and fun. They were also pretty tedious. While it's difficult to say they prepared us for what was ahead, I'm not sure anything really could have. Once we found out our sites, most of us mentally checked out. I remember Keith standing up in the middle of one of the classes, muttering, "I'm sick of this bullshit," and walking out. His wife, Cathy, turned red as a bowl of borscht and rolled her eyes. Keith was an older retiree, and about the only one of us who could've gotten away with that.

The class with the most utility was the Russian language class. My teacher, Ludmilla Anatolovna, believed in experiential learning. Early on, she marched our class down to the *rynok*, the open-air market where you could find just about anything for sale. There's one in every town and they can be super fascinating. I was taking it all in, looking at nothing in particular, when I heard Ludmilla Anatolovna's voice.

"*Dooglas*, go buy some plums."

"What?"

"Plums. Go buy some."

I saw a stall piled high with various fruits and approached it. I grabbed a plum and asked the seller how much it was. As I was talking with the guy, and trying to conceive in my mind how many plums there are in a kilogram, Ludmilla Anatolovna suddenly appeared over my shoulder and ordered me to haggle with him, telling me that unless he dropped what amounted to ten cents off the price, we'd walk.

"What?"

"Cheaper, *Dooglas*, cheaper."

"But why?"

"Do it."

What ensued was an embarrassed half-hearted back and forth negotiation over a fruit I don't particularly like, the vendor - a young kid from Central Asia who clearly didn't sign up for this - trying to maintain his precarious bottom line, and Ludmilla Anatolovna vigorously egging me on, telling me I wasn't doing it right - *Cheaper, Dooglas, cheaper.* The implication was that if I couldn't handle this, Russia was going to eat me alive.

Eventually I closed the deal within the financial parameters Ludmilla Anatolovna had established and handed the bag of plums to her.

She asked if wanted any.

"No."

I never again negotiated at a *rynok*. The *babushki* in Vladimir could've set the price of an orange at forty dollars and I probably would've paid it.

*

I ain't gonna fall for you
Like the temperature outside
I'll stand taller than the mercury
Till this chill subsides.

And the leaves will turn
And they'll fall too
Just like
They always do

And when we're found
Lying on the ground,
Yeah, I guess that I'll fall too

But not for you.

I wrote this sitting on the bed in my bedroom in Zelenograd. My host family, Valentin and Tamara Sergeev, had a guitar in the spare bedroom I lived in. It was a welcome bit of serendipity. Their apartment was pretty standard, small, in a tower block in the Fourteenth Microregion of Zelenograd, not far from the Kryukovo rail station that had been the center of the original village that Zelenograd swallowed up when it was founded. The apartment was on about the tenth floor. I used to gaze out the window at an identical tower block across the courtyard. I wondered if the occupants were gazing back, but they had probably internalized the reflection to the point that they didn't notice it anymore. There were about a half dozen of these towers in a row, like a row of concrete dominos. It was as if two mirrors were placed facing each other reflecting reflections into infinity.

Valentin and Tamara were older and retired. They had a daughter who lived nearby. She and her family came to visit a couple of times. Valentin had been an electrical engineer. He was well read. During one of our early conversations, I mentioned that a favorite book of mine was *Moscow-Petushki* by Venedikt Erofeev. Valentin not only knew the book but had an unfavorable opinion of it. It wasn't the only time he offered literary criticism. When some of the students I worked with in Zelenograd gave me a volume of Pushkin, Valentin made a show of telling me that, while Pushkin was good - you can never say a bad word about Pushkin - he preferred Lermontov. When I went out to site in October, his parting gift to me was a two-volume anthology of Lermontov.

Valentin was also pretty handy. Once we were heading out somewhere in his red Lada. The car wouldn't start, so he went to the trunk and returned with a ball peen hammer. He bashed the hammer a few times on the engine block, turned the key, and it started right up. Amazing.

I often wondered what Valentin made of me. He was taciturn, and I filled in the blanks and assumed that he didn't think much of me. We used to take long, wordless walks around Zelenograd. I would try to make small talk but it didn't amount to much. I wondered if I was an annoyance. I remember one of the first nights I was there, Valentin looking at me with increasing frustration as I labored to eat the roasted chicken on my plate with a knife and fork. He finally ran out of patience and glared at me before saying «С руками! С руками!» which literally means "Use your hands!" but strongly implied "God damn it!" as a preface. For all the doubts I had, I came to believe that this was just his nature. I remember him being jovial the night of our reception at the end of Training. I have a picture of him and me and Tamara, and he has a genuine, if faint, smile on his face.

Tamara was an old grandmother. She was sweet and intense. When I got a bad cold sometime in September, she mustered all of her Russian *babushka* skills in an effort to get me on the mend. All I wanted was to be left alone, to convalesce in peace, but that wasn't an option. She plastered my chest with hot compresses and forced me to drink several elixirs of her own making. I still have an image in my mind of her silhouetted by the light coming in to my darkened room from the hallway, rhythmically chanting "Пей! Пей! Пей! Пей! Пей!" - "Drink! Drink!" - swinging her arms as if beating a drum, as I struggled to down the hot tonic she had given me without scalding myself.

I also remember Tamara grabbing me by the wrist and pulling me into the apartment as I fumbled the keys trying to open the door on the afternoon of September 11th, oblivious to what was happening. With one motion she flung me like we were figure skating partners through the door and into the bedroom where the TV was. As I sat there speechless, she placed a bowl of borscht on a table in front of me. I scalded myself that day too.

When I left the apartment for the final time as I headed out to site, Tamara gave me a big kiss on the lips, grabbing both of my cheeks with her thick, Slavic, calloused hands. I can still see her waving as the elevator door closed.

***

The Irony of Fate

Interlude: The Toughest Job You'll Ever Love

I remember how utterly alone I felt when the students from the college and Anya and Polina left that first night in Vladimir. I remember warming up the pork chops that Tamara sent with me. I remember reading *Novel with Cocaine* those first few weeks. I remember making arrangements while on the train in transit to meet with Melanie at the Golden Gate a few days after we arrived. I remember her welcoming party at the *vokzal* was much bigger than mine.

*

If I were a believer in fate, I'd say it had something to do with me being sent to Vladimir.

I had actually been there before, on my first trip to the Soviet Union in 1991. It had been added to the itinerary almost as an afterthought. In years past, the school trip I was lucky enough to go on had included stops in Tallinn or Kyiv, in addition to Moscow and Leningrad. In the tumult of the early 1990s, as the country was imploding, it seemed safer to stay within the Russian Republic, so we went to Vladimir and Suzdal instead.

The town didn't make much of an impression on me. Where are all the grand palaces? Where's the Soviet kitsch? It was just a bunch of old churches covered in grime. Of all the photographs my mother and I took on that trip, there isn't a single one from Vladimir.

What I wouldn't give for a photograph of a thirteen-year old me standing in front of the Golden Gate.

Ten years later, as I was trying to find a way to get back to Russia after my semester in St. Petersburg, I considered applying for work at the American Home. There were several reasons why I didn't pursue it further, but one of them was the lingering non-memory of Vladimir.

"I've been there before, why would I want to go back?"

The Irony of Fate.

*

About a month after we arrived in Zelenograd, we found out where our sites were going to be. There had been a bit of an anticipatory buildup to this. Over the previous couple of weeks, I had sent several emails to my parents telling them that there were "rumors" that our assignments were imminent. I began to feel a nervous excitement. A life that was heretofore theoretical was about to be defined, the contours formed, the images sharpened.

I don't really know what I was expecting with respect to my assignment. I had wishful thoughts about being posted near St. Petersburg, naively thinking I could recreate the exhilarative life of my recent semester there. I remember telling the Peace Corps staff that being sent to Siberia was "overwhelming," but that I'd be fine if that's where I wound up. In truth, I'd be fine wherever they sent me. Everything was ill-defined, and that was how it should have been. It was time to define it.

But it was initially a bit of a letdown when I found out I was being sent to Vladimir. Of all the places in Russia, of all of the cities and towns and villages stretched out over the largest country on earth, I was being sent to a place I had been before. When I told Tamara later that day, she sighed and said «Близко» - "That's close." She seemed unimpressed too.

Despite this initial misgiving, I emailed home to my parents that though it was "sort of anticlimactic," I was excited. And I was. True, it was close, and I had been there before, and maybe it wasn't sexy and "exotic." But now I could focus on the future. I could start imagining the life I had been attempting to build for the previous two years.

My story at long last had a setting.

Vladimir.

Поехали.

*

Sitting on my bookshelf is a copy of M. Ageyev's *Novel with Cocaine.* The spine is in good shape, with only a small blemish on the top corner. There are no markings in the book, nothing underlined, no notes in the margins, no corners folded down. Its only other imperfection is where I had written my name on the title page, indicating that I bought it on October 11, 2001, at Angliya, a bookshop in Moscow. There's a price sticker on the back: 400 rubles. Tucked into the back cover is a page from a day-by-day calendar.

October 31, 2001.

The day I arrived in Vladimir.

When Anya and Polina and a few students from the college where I was to work deposited me in my room after I arrived that night, I made myself something to eat, took a deep breath, grabbed the book, and ripped off the page from the calendar to use as a bookmark. I lay down on the bed. Before opening the book, I took in my surroundings.

My new home was about fifteen by fifteen. There were two beds, a desk, several chairs and two cabinets. There was a small closet with a couple of shelves. On the pale green wallpaper by the door, there was a dusty Chuck Taylor footprint, no doubt the remnants of one of the eager students from the college who helped prepare the room for my arrival. Every once in a while, the overhead light flickered.

I tried to read but I couldn't concentrate on the book, that night, or afterwards, blindly turning pages, scanning words, my thoughts not on Ageyev's plot or characters, instead engrossed in the story I was living, the first chapter of which had just begun. I had no idea where the story was going to lead.

I'd just have to keep reading.

*

Interlude: Троллейбус, Который Идёт На Восток

Soon after arriving in Vladimir, I asked one of my colleagues if there was a map of the various bus and trolleybus routes I could buy to help me get around. She said no such map existed, but suggested riding around the busses with a pencil and paper and drawing one myself.

*

Vladimir was a pretty happening place in the twelfth century.

In its heyday, it had become the locus of power as Kievan Rus' shifted to the northeast. While Moscow was little more than a backwater, Vladimir was a cosmopolitan capital, importing architects and masons from Europe to design and build its grand cathedrals and palaces. Vladimir's position of dominance in the region was confirmed when Andrei Bogolyubsky, the Grand Prince of Vladimir-Suzdal, in an act of veritable matricide, sent an army from Vladimir to sack Kyiv in 1169. The destruction of Kyiv came after Andrei had already plundered many of its treasures, including the venerated Byzantine icon that was to become known as Our Lady of Vladimir, which became one of the most significant cultural and religious artifacts in Russian history. Andrei ordered the construction of the Assumption Cathedral in Vladimir to house it. Over time, the icon came to be seen as something of a Russian palladium, holding seemingly miraculous powers, and was credited with warding off attacks from Timur Tamerlane in 1395 and the Fascists in 1941.

However, whatever supernatural protective abilities it may or may not have possessed weren't enough to prevent the Mongols under Batu Khan from sacking Vladimir in 1238, and the city never quite recovered from this calamity. Although it nominally remained the capital of what would become Russia, its power and influence was diminished, and over time it became just one of a dozen of ancient towns ringing Moscow, the new center of gravity. Eventually, as the final insult, Moscow removed Our Lady of Vladimir from the city, and constructed its own Assumption Cathedral, modeled after the one in Vladimir, in which to house it.

I lived about a half mile west of the city center. My building was tucked back from Prospekt Lenina, the main boulevard that ran through downtown. I'd access it by walking through an alleyway lined with garages. In my immediate neighborhood was the Hotel Zarya, a concert hall, and a couple of small *produkty,* corner grocery stores where I bought most of my food.

Prospekt Lenina took a slight turn at the Hotel Zarya, and shortly thereafter turned again, at which point it became Ulitsa Bolshaya Moskovskaya, which was its name as it ran through the center of the city. From here, you could see down the avenue to the Golden Gate, the twelfth century entrance to the old city. Beyond that were the 900-year old cathedrals for which Vladimir is known, the Cathedral of St. Dmitrius and the imposing Assumption Cathedral.

Melanie lived northwest of the city center, near the university. From there, an arc of newer development enclosed the historic core. The college where I worked was just outside downtown, wedged behind a large city park and a mid-century residential complex. Along the railroad tracks on the east side of the city was an industrial zone, with chemical plants and the power station. Eventually, like all Russian cities, Vladimir became apartment blocks stacked side by side by side.

That was it. That was the city. It wasn't terribly impressive. After Simon came to visit us that winter, he wrote:

Vladimir is not a lovely city . . . It is, like many other cities in Russia, industrial: uninspired apartment buildings, factories, a nuclear [sic] power plant, and so on. It is not without its charm, but its charm is limited.

When I read Simon's impressions, I took a bit of offense, but I couldn't argue with him that much. I counseled my parents when they were planning a trip to come visit me that they shouldn't plan to spend too much time in Vladimir because it takes "about two hours to see everything interesting." Like endless rows upon rows of identical concrete blocks, Vladimir was just like a hundred mid-sized Russian industrial cities. You've seen one, you've seen them all.

I don't blame my thirteen-year old self for being unimpressed with it.

Its charm is limited.

*

Vladimir may not have had obvious charm, but one thing it did have was Ludmilla Anatolovna, my language teacher from Training who, by coincidence, was from Vladimir.

Having Ludmilla Anatolovna in Vladimir was like having a mother in town, and there's no way that the fee I paid her for the weekly language classes was fair compensation for all she did for me. Upon my arrival she took me shopping for the basics: some towels and sheets, a basin in which to wash my clothes, some clothes hangers on which they could dry. She scoped out a place in town where I could buy a guitar, and upon hearing me lament the state of the kitchen in my dormitory, she loudly complained on my behalf to the college where I worked. While this put me in a bit of a difficult position - the ungrateful, entitled American who was too good for the given accommodations - the motives behind it were right. It's not something I asked for, but it was nice to know there was a *babushka* who would unleash herself on my behalf if anything called for it.

If her skills could be deployed strategically, it was a great thing to have in your corner. Memories of the Zelenograd *rynok* aside, when Ludmilla Anatolovna offered to take me shopping for winter clothes, I jumped at the chance, though I probably couldn't have said no if I had wanted to. As always, there was a bit of a preface, as she had judged the winter coat I had as entirely unsatisfactory, with a dismissive backhanded compliment of it being a nice "fall coat." Perhaps with thoughts of my belabored negotiations over plums in her mind, perhaps just with the perpetual determination not to take anyone's shit, she led the way, and within an hour of our arrival at the *rynok*, I was decked out with a knock-off Umbro down parka, a leather and wool hat with ear flaps, and a pair of gloves made of at least two different animals. That she acquired these things for around a thousand rubles - about thirty bucks - is a testament to the steamroller she was.

My language classes at her apartment were lengthy affairs. I'd ride the bus to the outer reaches of the city, away from the historic core where I lived, to an endless sea of Brezhnev-era high rises that lined Suzdalsky Prospekt. I'd always try to work my way to the back of the crammed bus and stare out the window as it traversed the backbone of the city - Prospekt Lenina, Bolshaya Moskovskaya,

Bolshaya Nizhegorodskaya, the alternating names of the street that was once known as the Vladimirka, the road that led, eventually, to Siberia. I'd watch the city pass by - the Golden Gate, the Assumption Cathedral, the Cathedral of St. Demetrius, the white walls of the Bogoroditse-Rozhdestvensky Monastery, Vladimirsky Tsentral prison, the power station, the chemical plant that had been awarded the Order of the Red Banner of Labor. I would disembark from the bus and trudge across the courtyard to her building, ascend the elevator, and ring the bell. When she opened the door I would be greeted with the hearty scents of rich Eastern Slavic cuisine.

Before the lesson, it was time for lunch.

We'd sit at the kitchen table and eat and talk. After we ate, we had tea. She taught me how to drink tea the Russian way, sweetened with *varenye*, or with a sugar cube clenched between your teeth. And we'd talk more. She'd tell me about how she remembered crying when Stalin died, and about her days as a Russian instructor in Soviet-occupied Hungary, where she learned to make the delicious goulash she often served me.

Her husband, Slava, was occasionally there too. He was as jovial and understated as she was energetic. One time that spring, as I described with excitement how I was looking forward to teaching at Lake Baikal in the summer, peppering my description with frequent usage of the words "Siberia" and "camp," he interrupted me.

"*Dooglas, please* - when talking about camps in Siberia, say '*пионерский лагерь*' (scout camp)."

Oh.

Right.

After tea, she'd make me a cup of Nescafé and the lesson would begin. I had vocabulary lists to memorize, sure, but mostly it was just us talking, about my life in Vladimir, about the Tarkovsky films we watched, about politics, about Russia, and America, and Russia *and* America. After an hour or so of this, she'd send me on my way. All told, an ostensible hour-long lesson usually lasted upwards of three.

I had a lot of people who were incredibly generous to me in Vladimir, but Ludmilla Anatolovna was like my protector, my guardian, my own personal Our Lady of Vladimir icon. As I left her apartment for the last time before I moved to Ekaterinburg, she grabbed me by the shoulders, made the sign of the cross over me, kissed me on both cheeks, and gave me a hug.

I'll never be able to repay her.

*

Interlude: Lost in Translation

I usually told people that I went to college "near Chicago" because the name of my university means "I am farting" in Russian. Somehow this never came up in eight semesters of Russian classes.

*

Hey Laura Jean
Yeah, you're driving me to murder
With those sad songs
That you think you've got to play

Hey Laura Jean
You should take some time to notice
That those songs you sing
They don't have to be this way

-       Vladimir, 2001

I wrote this in my room in Vladimir, shortly after my arrival. There was at least one more verse to this song but I can't remember it. It was a bouncy minor chord affair that I kind of liked, but it didn't do much as a song, and I don't think I ever played it for anybody.

"Laura Jean" is my friend Laura. During that first fall, Laura often served as a subject for me to project song ideas on, and that's what I was doing here. Laura was certainly not "sad"; she radiated a *joie de vivre* that was intoxicating, but I needed a subject and called on my pal Laura.

Writing "about" Laura was at least in part a recognition that I was suddenly separated from so many people I had grown so close to in such a short period of time. After Training, our group was dispatched over a geographical expanse that stretched 2,700 miles from west to east, which is greater than the distance from New York to Los Angeles. Friends whom I had seen every day for two months were now hundreds - if not thousands - of miles away. Laura was in Penza. Adam was in Volgograd. Chris was in Verkhoturye. Simon was in Aginskoye. Andrew and Rob were in Krasnoyarsk. We kept up with each other to the extent that we could, but email chains were a poor substitute for drinking beers down by the lake, or bumming around Moscow on a Saturday. Once we arrived at site, we all had to figure out a way to get our bearings without so many of the people we had depended on the first couple of months in Zelenograd.

But I was lucky.

I had Melanie.

My songs didn't have to be sad.

*

Interlude: Слава Труду!

I went to the Vladimir Tractor Factory, named for Zhdanov, recipient of the Order of the Red Banner of Labor, soon after arriving. There were things about it that were unsafe.

*

It a little windy in this city
God breath so hard it hard to stand
We walk along all down the sidewalk
She grab my sleeve she grab my hand

And she knows what to do when she feels lonely
And she knows what to do when she feels sad

-       Vladimir, 2001

This had a couple more verses. The whole thing was written ungrammatically. I guess I thought it would be cool to have an ungrammatical verse and then grammatical chorus. I don't recall where I got that idea or why I thought it was a good one. It might have come from thinking about my own Russian, and what I may have sounded like to all my new neighbors. But I didn't think about that possibility until recently.

The reference to the wind was a comment on the onset of winter. I remember it snowing in Vladimir the night I arrived. I remember walking up and down the platform looking for a familiar face after I disembarked from the train. I remember the snowflakes bouncing off of Anya's pale blue hat as I saw her.

Anya and Polina were my closest friends from work. Anya had a melancholy about her, but it was tempered by a bit of a madcap streak. My favorite memory of Anya is the time we went out to Bogolyubovo for a picnic sometime in the spring of 2002. We spent a wonderfully carefree day wandering in the fields next to the Church of the Intercession on the Nerl, building a fire, climbing trees. We cooked sausages and drank beer. It was a perfect day.

The aimless quality of this activity was typical. We used to take long walks after school, both of us sort of heading the same way, sort of not, but eager for company before one of us invariably caught a bus going in the other direction. Our interactions were refreshingly unpretentious. One of my greatest regrets is that my leaving Vladimir interrupted our friendship and I never got to say a proper goodbye.

Polina was my counterpart at the college in Vladimir. I liked Polina from the moment I met her at a reception in

Moscow at which we were introduced before going out to site. So many small, seemingly meaningless vignettes about her are lodged in my memory. I remember how she mixed her red wine with a bottle of carbonated water at the reception the night we met. Later, while walking around the city getting to know each other, we dropped into the Cathedral of Christ the Savior, as if to get a blessing. I certainly needed it. I remember her gazing up wide-eyed at the iconostasis as she crossed herself. Waiting for our train to take us to Vladimir for my site visit a couple of days later, she seemed bothered by the fact that I was wearing a *telnyashka* that Tamara had given me to replace the tattered long sleeve undershirts that I had been wearing as it got colder. I didn't take the *telnyashka* to be anything other than a normal shirt, but Polina pointed out that it was definitely not meant to be worn out in public, with a tone of voice suggesting that fatal Russian putdown, that I was «некультурный» - "uncultured," but carrying the implication that one is scarcely more than a savage. It's safe to say that Tamara was sending a similar message about my некультурность and that this shirt was a step up from my previous wardrobe, but that's another matter. Later, in Vladimir, when Polina noticed me continually taking my hat off as we dropped into various shops getting things for my dormitory, she paradoxically asked if I was "some sort of aristocrat."

Despite critiquing my sensibilities, Polina was always very generous, checking in on me and asking how I was doing, perhaps feeling that I was in over my head. She took me under her wing from that very first night in Moscow, when, as we were parting, she insisted we figure out a way for me to contact her and assure her I had made it back to

Zelenograd alive. Despite my assurance that I would be fine, she wouldn't take no for an answer. It was all very sweet. She got these maternal instincts from her mother, who was absolutely delightful, like a character out of Voinovich, possessed with an earthy warmth and a frivolity that I always adored. Their apartment, in a *khrushchyovka* on the other side of town from where I lived, was always warm and welcoming.

The cold, strong wind was ever-present during those first few weeks in Vladimir. It rained and snowed enough to trigger the infamous Russian *rasputitsa*, though it didn't get cold enough to freeze consistently until late November or December. But that was just the beginning. A mental turning point for me came one day in January. I remember having the thought that minus twenty-five degrees Celsius was a relatively warm day.

This was a pretty early one, probably November 2001. Laura makes an appearance in this song too, as I imagined her being the one who grabbed my arm to steady herself in the wind.

*

I was assigned to teach at the Vladimir Pedagogical College. It served recent graduates of secondary school who planned to become English teachers, or perhaps work in tourism. Polina and Anya and a couple of other teachers there were alumnae of the college. The course of study lasted three years, at which point the students could apply for admission to university, or join the workforce. It seemed a bit like junior college to me. Most of the students lived at home, and just about all of them were women.

The college was located on Ulitsa Poliny Osipenko, a leafy street tucked behind the 850th Anniversary of Vladimir Park. The park abutted the city *rynok*, stretching about a quarter of a mile along Ulitsa Mira, a boulevard that bisected the northeastern part of the city center. I'd usually take a bus through the old town and get off at the *rynok*, before cutting through the park to get to the college. Sometimes I'd walk down Ulitsa Mira, the cars whizzing past. The college was not big, contained entirely within a two-story building made up of a central hall and two wings that extended away from the street. There was a small library where I could borrow materials for teaching, and a mid-sized auditorium on the second floor.

I'm not sure what the students or faculty made of my arrival, but just about everyone was nice. I was assigned to teach several sections of speech practice. Most of my students had a decent handle on English, which was a good thing, as my pedagogical shortcomings were evident from the start.

I was a curiosity to most of my students. A lot of them had seen an American before – Vladimir is a pretty standard destination for tour packages traveling along the "Golden Ring," a circle of quaint historic towns within driving distance from Moscow - but I was certainly the first they had sustained contact with. They weren't that much younger than me, and had memories of the end of the Cold War from the Soviet perspective. There was still an excitement about Russians and Americans interacting with each other, as if it was a touch forbidden or edgy, and here I was, a real American specimen dropped into their little college on Ulitsa Poliny Osipenko.

This meant there was a bit of fluidity between my work life and my normal life in Vladimir, particularly during those first few months. To an extent, I was always "on." I wasn't just a guy wandering into the *produkty* to buy groceries. I was The American. I wasn't just the new teacher at Vladimir Pedagogical College. I was The American Teacher, The Volunteer. I didn't mind this, but it did mean I was never really off the job. Even when I wasn't teaching, I was still The American. Of course, this was one of the purposes of being a Peace Corps Volunteer, to serve as a living, breathing emissary of the United States, dispatched to counter images of The Ugly American. If I was sometimes annoyed by all of this attention, it was coming from a good place. Several of my students knew where I lived, and would show up and ask me to hang out with them. There were boundaries to this of course, but the students and I were basically the same age, and I enjoyed spending time with them within certain parameters.

There was a group of third year students who were especially friendly. They were in one of my advanced classes and seemed to move as a five-headed monster, four girls – Nastya, Dasha, Zhenya and Marina – and a guy – Semyon. Semyon's English was the best of all of them. He spoke with a touch of a Mancunian accent, which he picked up by mimicking Noel Gallagher, singing Oasis songs when he had a guitar handy – which was often – or just by saying "*fook*" a lot.

Of the others, Dasha and Nastya were the most sociable. Marina was quiet and reserved, and Zhenya had a whimsy about her that was charming. They'd invite me to go for walks around the city when the weather was nice, or try to cajole me into going to a club with them. They did this because they were nice, but I always felt to a degree that it was also because I was a curio, a novelty, that this was obviously something they wouldn't be doing with their other instructors. I felt at times that I couldn't say no, that this was as much a part of my job as the lessons I gave at the college, but it was still enjoyable. If I felt overwhelmed while in the classroom, this was an arena where I could be more useful and comfortable. I could play the part.

I wasn't much of a teacher. But I got pretty good at being The American.

*

Interlude: I Can See Clearly Now

I remember going to the top of the old water tower in Vladimir with one of my students, who was from Yakutsk. I remember her asking me if I had drunk vodka the night before. I lied and said no.

*

Screw your friends
Screw your world
Screw your parents
If it'll get you girls

Fight the Reds
Fight the Tories
Fight the Peace Corps
If it'll bring you glory

Anastasia when she closes her eyes
She sees sparkles in the sky
But they're not real
Anastasia when she opens her mouth
You hear the swear words rolling out
It's so surreal

Screw your neighbor
Screw his son
Screw his girlfriend
If she will give you some

Fight the Liberals
Fight the Teds
Fight Picasso
'Cause he wouldn't use red.

Anastasia when she closes her eyes
She sees sparkles in the sky
But they're not real
Anastasia when she opens her mouth
You hear the swear words rolling out
It's so surreal

-        Vladimir, 2001

This is an early one, and a pretty stupid one at that. It was never a good song and I was happy when I wrote a lot of better songs and didn't have to play this one very much. If I had to defend it, I would say that it was a comment on the atomization of politics that seemed to be happening, finally, ten years after the Cold War ended and in the months after al-Qaeda loudly announced that there were going to be consequences for a half century of the bi-polar world treating most of the planet as a giant game of Risk. In addition to digesting the trauma of 9/11 and acting almost as an agent of a triumphant America dispatched to live among the vanquished former enemy, I remember reading about how politics seemed to be coming unglued, no longer bound by the norms of the old world. Hugo Chavez was treated as a comic anachronism in the pages of *Newsweek* whereas in years past he would have been painted as a Red Menace. More troublingly, a character like Pim Fortuyn seemed to square some of the circles of the traditional left-right split to an extent that put forth a defense of intolerance in the name of tolerance. I remember reading about him in the issues of *Newsweek International* that Peace Corps sent us and worrying that his brand of liberal bigotry was the wave of the future.

I wish I could have had a more profound digestion of these strands than this song, but this was what I came up with. I would sometimes sing it as "Fuck the Peace Corps" which was even dumber than what I wrote down. The Picasso line always embarrassed me. Like I said, this one wasn't very good.

The neighbor in this song was the guy who lived in the room next to mine in Vladimir. I can't remember his name. He was relatively short, with a round face and gray hair that matched the color of the sweater vest he often wore. My dormitory was attached to a teacher retraining institute. Teachers from the province would come to Vladimir from time to time for conferences, classes, trainings, and the like, and the building I lived in served as their accommodations. I was one of five permanent residents, all of whom lived in four rooms that connected to a common kitchen and bathroom. My next-door neighbor taught at the Institute. He had a teenage son who was sometimes there with him. He and I would drink vodka in the kitchen from time to time. I remember him expounding at length about how "logical" the Russian language was, and making a quip about Anna Akhmatova, that she was «Как Пушкин в юбке» - "Like Pushkin in a skirt."

Across the corridor were two women whom I never interacted with. I don't think I even knew their names. They were absolutely uninterested in who I was or what I was doing there, which was actually refreshing.

The last neighbor was also a teacher at the Institute. I can't remember her name either, but she was nice. I watched the Opening Ceremonies of the 2002 Winter Olympics with her and her teenage son, who was also there every once in a while.

That spring, she invited me to her birthday party. It was just her and her son and me. She had set the table with sweets and a bottle of Sovetskoe champagne. She giggled when the cork popped out of the bottle. She sang an old song as she poured:

Как здорово, что все мы здесь.
Сегодня собрались.

It translates as "How wonderful that we have all gathered here today," sort of like, "The gang's all here." It's supposed to be a joyful song, but it always sounded melancholy to me, played in the sad minor keys of Russian folk music, and her rendition was particularly maudlin. She reminded me of a Russian Eleanor Rigby, her singing serving as the face she kept in a jar by the door.

When I was moving out, I remember her asking me what was happening. I told her I was moving to Ekaterinburg. She looked at me, paused for a second, and said «Удачи Вам» - "good luck to you," using the formal construction - before retreating to her room and closing the door.

*

Interlude: Щи Да Каша — Пища Наша

I would go to the *pirozhki* place on Bolshaya Moskovskaya before heading over to the college. The staff recognized me.

*

The sun's gonna shine down on thee
The sun's gonna shine down on thee
The sun's gonna shine down on thee
The sun ain't gonna shine down on me

So viva America!
Viva this glass of wine!
Viva unconsciousness!
Viva viva this turpentine!

Grace is gonna bless your touch
Grace is gonna bless your touch

Grace is gonna bless your touch
Grace gonna treat me a little rough

So viva America!
Viva this glass of wine!
Viva unconsciousness!
Viva viva this turpentine!

-       Vladimir, 2001

This one isn't very good either. I remember feeling in the winter of 2001-2002 that the sympathy much of the world felt for the United States after 9/11 was fading, and that our grief had morphed into a desire for vengeance. An ironic "Viva America" seemed appropriate.

This one was pretty simple, and could be fun to play - it actually had a riff in the middle! - but apart from that, there's not much going on here.

As an American in Russia, I was an object of curiosity for a while, until everybody got used to me and then I became decidedly less interesting. Hearing my accent, I was often asked where I was from, and when I answered, that was usually the end of it. Saying I was from Canada or Germany or wherever would have gotten the same response.

My neighbors' views of *America* as a concept were of course a little more complicated, but even then, they seemed to operate within predictable and fairly innocuous parameters. There was a bit of a post-Cold War optimism about former enemies becoming friends, tempered with the effects of the neoliberal shock therapy of the 1990s that many Russians blamed for the woes the country faced in the early 2000s. We sometimes served as a target for both impulses. This manifested itself in random Russians insisting on drinking vodka with me just because I was an American, but it also meant I had to answer for anything that America did, from a weird trade dispute involving steel and chicken legs to the march to war in Iraq.

There were a few instances of Russians acting out against the US that I witnessed. During the Winter Olympics in 2002, there was a figure skating scandal that put the USA and Russia on opposite sides of a cheating dispute. I never understood what the whole thing was about, but it really struck a nerve in Vladimir. Some residents decided the best course of action was to lash out at the most convenient symbol of the USA in town, and so they egged the American Home, before scrawling "Fuck You Salt Lake City" in English on the vinyl siding. Later that year, I was in St. Petersburg on May Day when I saw a crowd set an American flag on fire in the middle of Nevsky Prospekt. I got out of there, but wasn't too concerned. If you're not setting an American flag ablaze during a May Day parade, you're doing it wrong.

However, the memory that sticks with me the most is from the weekend after September 11th. A bunch of Volunteers went into Moscow. We had heard that there was a makeshift memorial near the American Embassy and we wanted to go see it. I'll never forget rounding the corner on Novinsky Bulvar and seeing the sidewalk, stretching about 300 feet along the facade of the embassy complex, covered in flowers, grouped in pairs, the traditional Russian way of expressing mourning. It was almost overwhelming.

*

Interlude: An Even Number of Flowers

I remember riding in a trolleybus on a snowy night as it traveled down Bolshaya Moskovskaya past the Bogoroditse-Rozhdestvensky Monastery sometime in November 2001. Suddenly, the conductor slammed on the brakes and the trolleybus skidded for a time until there was a loud bang and we came to a halt. The side doors opened and we all started filing out into the snowy night. The guy we had just hit lay lifeless in the snow in front of the trolleybus.

*

Me and Mac make a pretty good team
She'll play the heart and I'll play the spleen
And I beg the Lord that she'll never be
Remotely like me
Hopeless like me
Unfocused like me
And that she'll learn not to hide from the world
Learn not to run for the hills
Learn some things that she can teach to me

-      Vladimir, 2001

Around Thanksgiving, my niece Mackenzie was born. I spent the next year and a half looking forward to meeting her. I remember this song had a cool guitar part, but I don't remember how to play it anymore.

*

Interlude: Isn't It A Pity

I remember sitting in the auditorium upstairs at the College, going through a bunch of mail the Moscow office sent me, reading in *Newsweek* that George Harrison had died. It wasn't the most traumatic event that year, but I was upset nonetheless.

*

The American Home was one of Vladimir's peculiarities. A suburban tract house built by a misguided American entrepreneur in the '90s, it stood at the base of what remained of the old city walls. The armies of Batu Khan likely amassed on that exact spot in February 1238, as they attacked the Golden Gate, the main entrance to the city, on their way to burning Vladimir to the ground and massacring its inhabitants. When the house was constructed 750 years later, Vladimir was in a similarly difficult - though perhaps less dramatic - place after the collapse of the Soviet Union. If the idea was that it would be the first of many ranch houses constructed in the city, an imagined Levittown-on-the-Klyazma, the concept didn't take off. At some point, the house was repurposed as a school, importing Americans to teach English instead of granite countertops and refrigerators with ice dispensers.

Polina presented the American Home as a selling point when she was telling me about Vladimir, as if I really had the option of rejecting the place, but it was nice to know that it was there as I prepared myself for the move. Melanie, Ludmilla Anatolovna, the American Home; I was all about safety nets, so entrenched and real was the trepidation and anxiety I felt that had an uneasy balance with the excitement for what was to come.

Melanie and I were welcomed right away. We spent Thanksgiving at the American Home a few weeks after our arrival. Someone who worked there had gone into Moscow, bought a turkey, lugged the thing all the way back to Vladimir on a train, and had graciously invited Melanie and me to share some of it. It was incredibly generous.

We became part of the group. There were seven American teachers there, most of them about our age, all of them in the same milieu. I started seeing one of them, Liz. It was an intense relationship at an intense time. From then on, my relationship to the American Home followed the contours of my relationship with Liz. Once it ended, so too did my relationship with the American Home.

It's always been weird to me that had I pursued work there further, I would have met so many of those same people on a different astral plane.

The Irony of Fate

*

Let's take baby steps 1-2-3
We won't get married inevitably
This might be just a fling
Or it might be something

I love what we do on those lazy afternoons
The sun is shining bright
And it might keep on
Shining through the night

I'd like to hang your canvas up on my wall
And turn this room into a gallery hall
'Cause those colors yeah they suit you good
And I'd paint you if I could

Who knows what it took
To capture that look
And I may not have the right
To paint you pastel yellow tonight

-       Vladimir, probably 2002, maybe 2001

*

Under blankets and quilts
Winter will repent
With the warmth of your touch
As our recompense

With the kiss of your breath

All smack'd on my cheeks
I could hide from this chill
By your side for weeks

And though our skin may not fuse
If we press it as such
Such a goal one might think
From the length of our touch

And if lying all winter
Isn't quite what we do
We'll be warmer together
Lying sideways, we two.

-        Vladimir, probably 2002, maybe 2001

*

Sweet tea
For thee
Cold hands
And sympathy

The world's gonna look out for you

-        Vladimir, probably 2002, maybe 2001

*

Don't laugh when you kiss me
I know it seems strange
To stand here a-shivering
Parting as the day begins

We're buried in sweaters
In scarves gloves and coats
As our breath drifts above us
A halo that heavenward floats

Darlin' you're sweeter than the tea that I drink
You make fun of me with a smile and a wink
Still it's in my nature to wait for this ship to sink

And your touch warms my hands
My fingers my toes
Though last time I checked
It was 30 below

Let's go back inside
Escape the chill of the street
And we'll lie arm in arm
An advance and not a retreat

Darlin' you're sweeter than the tea that I drink
You make fun of me with a smile and a wink
Still it's in my nature to wait for this ship to sink

-       Vladimir, 2002

My relationship with Liz was sweet. That may or may not have been why it didn't last, but that's what it was. Liz essentially lived across the street. We could walk doorstep to doorstep in three minutes: down the alley, past the Hotel Zarya, cross the crosswalk to the concert hall, turn left, next building, pink mortar, entrance around back. I was usually rushing in any event, so three minutes might be overestimating a bit. Our relationship was also pretty intense. Spend-every-waking-second-together-and-ache-when-you're-not-together intense. That either made it the first adult relationship I had or the last adolescent one. At the time, for what it was, it was pretty great. This is a document of me walking her home for the first time. Even in the midst of it, I guess I sensed a shelf life.

I've never been able to find a song structure that I like for this one. I've tried different time signatures and tempos, messed around with the chords, and it's never quite fit. But I do like the words for the most part even if they're a bit slight, especially in the refrain.

This song and the verses before it are also yet another documentation of the winter. I wasn't a total stranger to the cold. There were a few times growing up, certainly lots more in college, and the last month or so I spent in St. Petersburg when I had had a taste of the extreme cold. Still, it wasn't anything like that first winter in Vladimir, which itself paled in comparison to the next in the Urals, and it certainly made an impression on me.

In the depths of winter, I would put on an absurd number of layers to go outside. I had to get a vaccination in Ekaterinburg sometime in the winter of 2002-2003. Peace Corps had arranged for me to get it in a clinic across the courtyard from my building. It took several minutes to wrap myself in insulation - parka on top of sweater on top of shirt on top of thermal, to say nothing of two scarves and two pairs of gloves, the thicker of which was essentially a rabbit that I stuck on my hands. All this to trudge 100 feet through the snow, spend another five minutes unwrapping myself, just to get a prick with a needle, before repeating the process in reverse.

It was all necessary though. On an especially cold Saturday in December 2002 or January 2003, when the temperature dropped to about minus forty, I went for a walk in the city, much to the chagrin of Elena Ivanovna, my supervisor at the university. As I emerged from the subway downtown, I realized I was in for something I hadn't fully anticipated. I remember actually feeling my body weaken as I walked. I had to drop into storefronts periodically to warm up, seemingly so my metabolism wouldn't cease and I'd lose all ability to function. It was a distinct physical sensation, as if someone had opened up a spigot at my ankle and the energy was draining out of me, pooling at my feet.

It was around this time that I purchased a thermometer which I stuck outside my window so I could monitor the extremes that winter was presenting me, as if I were the caretaker and record keeper at an Arctic meteorological outpost. Silly me didn't account for the permanent layer of frost affixed to the window panes, obscuring any data I may have hoped to record.

More practically, the cold would render the room-temperature bottles of beer I bought at the shop across the street cold enough to drink by the time I got home. And if they weren't quite ready, hanging the bag outside of the window would finish the job in a minute or two.

*

Interlude: Winterlude

I used to slide down the exposed sheets of ice that kids would make on the sidewalk in the winter.

*

Everyone once in a while, I convened an English Club at the college where I worked. A few students would show up, we'd drink tea, and converse on whatever topic was at hand. Everyone who attended was eager and enthusiastic, and I felt less pressure than during the course of my regular teaching responsibilities, when I was pretty constantly plagued by self-doubt. The students at the college were only a few years younger than me, and it was as much a social event as it was anything else.

During one meeting in December, we talked about Christmas songs. The holiday is a little different in Russia. Orthodox Christmas is in January, and the main event of the season is New Year's. The idea of so many songs about Christmas was a bit alien to them, but they were into it. I brought a songbook I had borrowed from the American Home, and we leafed through it. They'd choose a song, or I'd suggest one, we'd discuss the lyrics, I'd teach them the tune, we'd try our hand at singing it. I didn't have a guitar or anything. There were a lot of false starts and confusion and mixed up verses, but we muddled through it. It was fun.

We started with the classics. "Rudolph the Red-Nosed Reindeer." "Jingle Bells." "Deck the Halls." The students made jokes about Rudolph being a closet alcoholic and suggested that everyone was dashing through the snow on a Russian *troika*. They were excited, asking for more and more songs. "Frosty the Snowman" and "Silver Bells" and "O Christmas Tree." Soon their enthusiasm started exhausting the supply of songs that I knew. I was getting a little desperate when I told them about "White Christmas." I turned to the page in the songbook and we started going through it. I didn't get very far before one of the students spoke up.

"*Dooglas,* I not understand."

It was Lyosha. He was looking quizzically at the lyric sheet.

"Sure, Lyosha. What's up? Do you have a question about a word?"

"No, words I understand. But song not make sense."

"Ok?"

"*Catholic* Christmas is in December, yes?"

"The twenty-fifth, yes."

"And the song about hoping it snows?"

"Yes."

"At end of December?"

"Yes."

"Hoping it snows at end of December?"

I glanced out the window at the falling snow, which was falling on top of the snow that fell the day before, which lay on the snow that had fallen the day before, which lay on the...

"*Dooglas,* this song not make sense."

*

Interlude: Bear Any Burden, Meet Any Hardship

I remember sitting at the tiny kitchen table at my place in Vladimir reading *Kolyma Tales* and the *Lonely Planet Guide to Russia, Ukraine and Belarus.* I remember it took upwards of fifteen minutes to boil a kettle for coffee or tea. I remember hanging my laundry out to dry on the balcony off the common room, just outside my doorway. The clothes would freeze during the winter. My green, flannel sheets ripped as I peeled them off the line. I wound up later tearing these sheets (which I had had since college) into shreds to stuff between the cracks of the window panes in Ekaterinburg.

*

I don't think I was a model Peace Corps Volunteer. I didn't apply for any grants. I didn't come up with anything innovative at either of my sites. Maybe I was good at my teaching but maybe I wasn't. I don't really know. I arrived, I performed a role, and when I left, nothing was different.

If I was underwhelming in the basics of my job, Peace Corps must have seen something useful in me, as I was dispatched on a few occasions to various places for p.r. purposes. Ludmilla Anatolovna and I visited a school in Suzdal that had been unsuccessfully trying to land a Volunteer for a couple of years. We were sent to assure them to keep trying and not lose hope, and Ludmilla Anatolovna, as ever, had strong opinions on how this pitch should go. She made me take my guitar and insisted I play in front of a class. *Dooglas, please.* I wrote the chorus of "You've Got to Hide Your Love Away" on the chalkboard and led the students in a song. Young American showing up with a guitar to sing the Beatles to the Russians - I was a latter-day Samantha Smith. Or Dean Reed. My peacenik credentials were complete.

The most memorable of these forays was to Murom, a small city on the other side of Vladimirskaya Oblast'. I traveled there in April 2002. There was another Volunteer there, and he and I were supposed to lead a symposium on globalization at the local university. I didn't know anything about globalization, but we all sat around a table with little Russian and American flags, and I nodded and furrowed my brow a lot. Every once in a while, I said something that was a minor rephrasing of whatever comment someone else had made a few minutes before that seemed insightful. When it was over we all posed for pictures. I think it got written up in the local paper.

If the symposium was forgettable, the journey to Murom was really great. I got picked up in a Peace Corps Land Cruiser by Kolya and Elena. Kolya was one of the Peace Corps drivers, and Elena was essentially my boss. She was the Regional Program Manager for all sites north and east of Moscow stretching out to the Ural Mountains. My first impression of her was that she was stern and intimidating. She was quiet and didn't smile very much - that portrait of the humorless Russian. I hadn't interacted with her much up to that point, and when I had, it was very businesslike. I wasn't looking forward to the trip.

I loaded my stuff into the Land Cruiser and we set off. I sort of assumed that Kolya would drive through the center of town before turning onto the highway leading to

Murom, but he started off in the opposite direction. We drove up my street, Prospekt Lenina, and turned onto Builder's Street. Elena explained we were going to make one quick stop before we got on the road. We headed north from the city center towards the university where Melanie lived. I thought for a minute that maybe she was coming along too and I hadn't known about it. This became moot as we drove past the university. After a few minutes, Kolya parked the Land Cruiser. He and Elena got out so I followed them.

"*Dooglas,* did you bring a camera?" Elena asked.

I did and dug into my bag.

We crossed the street and I realized we were at Lenin Square. I had been there before but it was in a part of the city I didn't frequent.

"Give your camera to Kolya," said Elena.

Kolya held out his hand. He already had one camera.

"Ok," I said.

I followed Elena out onto the square. Lenin towered over us, one foot forward, a half step into a march. Lenin never just stands. He's always in action, pointing, gesturing, stabbing at the air. There's an old Soviet saying, "Ленин жил, Ленин жив, Ленин будет жить" - Lenin lived, Lenin lives, Lenin will always live. The statues erected in his honor seem to emphasize the second part.

Ленин жив.

Lenin lives.

Lenin is alive.

I looked over at Elena. She was posing just like Lenin. I laughed. She gestured for me to do the same. I did, looking up at Lenin and over at Elena to make sure my arm was at the right angle, whether I had the correct foot forward. As soon as I got the pose right, I heard a click. Kolya snapped a picture. Elena walked around to the other side and I followed. Kolya came towards us and he handed Elena a camera - not mine - and she motioned for Kolya and I to stand together at the base of the statue. She took a picture.

We milled around for a few minutes and then got back into the Land Cruiser. Kolya gave me my camera back. We drove back the way we came, turned onto the highway, and left the city behind us. For a couple of hours, we drove through the countryside. I remember passing an old collective farm, the optimistic slogan on the sign at its entrance long since faded. Soon the fields turned into forest, the road slicing through the trees.

The forest between Vladimir and Murom figures prominently in the folk history of the region. There are lots of tales about brigands and robbers accosting travelers on the very road we were driving down. The *bogatyr* Ilya Muromets, a mythical Russian folk hero, supposedly set out into the forest to confront the bandits on his way to fight their leader, Nightingale the Robber, an avian beast that terrorized medieval Rus' with a devilish whistle that could kill a man. When they faced each other, the creature stunned Ilya with the whistle, but he managed to survive and regain his wits, before ultimately decapitating Nightingale the Robber in a climactic battle that saved Rus'. At one point, Kolya pulled off on the side of the road next to a wooden house that had been accessorized with carvings of various fantastical creatures, a nightingale perched on the gable. It was like something out of a creepy fairy tale, like *The Raven*, with a heavy dose of Slavic exoticism.

As we approached Murom, I assumed they were going to drop me off at the other Volunteer's apartment and be done with me, but I was mistaken. Soon after entering the city, Kolya pulled the Land Cruiser to the shoulder. An olive drab armored locomotive was perched on a concrete plinth. Emblazoned on the side in white letters was the name "Ilya Muromets." During the war, the Soviets repurposed the fantastical tale of folklore to create a new narrative. Instead of fighting a mythical anthropomorphic bird, Ilya Muromets, like everybody, was sent to the front to fight the Fascists, blasting his way to Frankfurt an der Oder before V-E Day.

"*Dooglas*, give me your camera."

We got back in the Land Cruiser and turned into the grid of the downtown. We parked and walked the city streets. At the Lenin statue, Elena and I again imitated his pose, this time an outstretched hand and a clenched fist. At the base of the statue to Ilya Muromets, Kolya told me to triumphantly raise my arm, as Ilya himself was doing. We walked down the block to the ancient cathedral with the blue cupolas and then down the next to the ancient cathedral with the black cupolas.

At every stop, "*Dooglas*, give me your camera."

Murom is not a large city and I feel like we covered every street, every block. Both Kolya and Elena were Muscovites, but they were showing me around like they were locals. They wanted me to *see* it, to *remember* it. We happened to be in Murom, but I think they were treating this as a representation of Russia itself - the goofiness of the Lenin statues, the connections to the past, the folklore, the architecture. My photo album is filled with pictures of me on seemingly every block in the city.

"Dooglas, give me your camera."

I really enjoyed Elena's and Kolya's company. They had a warm banter between them, and they invited me into the conversation. They found it particularly funny when I would ask them about a Russian colloquialism I was unfamiliar with.

"What does 'халява' mean?"

"'Халява?' *Dooglas,* 'халява' means 'халява!'"

And they'd both roar with laughter.

Kolya was always gregarious, but I came to really appreciate Elena's sardonic wit and understated approach to life and her surroundings. I guess I didn't notice it until I saw her imitating Lenin in Vladimir. If at first I assumed that Elena was the dour Russian cliché, perhaps the Churchill quote about the riddle wrapped in a mystery inside an enigma is more appropriate, or, better, the one about the many-layered nesting dolls.

At the closing reception at Spaso House in February 2003, Elena handed me two photographs. They were from our trip to Murom the previous year. In the first, she and I are standing in front of the Lenin statue in Vladimir, imitating his pose. Despite my attempts to mimic Lenin's furrowed brow, I have a smirk on my face. Elena is stoic. She wrote on the back, "For a historian this man is a great mystery and Marxism-Leninism is a great challenge."

On the back of the second, she wrote, "With my appreciation to your attempts to fathom Marxism-Leninism from all angles." It's a picture of Kolya and me. We're standing together at the base of the Lenin statue.

Directly above us is his backside.

*

Interlude: Ленин жил

At the reception at Spaso House on the last night, a bunch of us were talking with Ivan, one of the Peace Corps drivers, about the travels we were about to embark on. We were heading in lots of different directions - to Oslo, to Croatia, to Poland. One of us asked, "Hey Ivan, have you ever been abroad?"

"Yes, I was in Prague. Long time ago."

"Cool! When?"

"1968."

"Oh. Wow. What did you do there?"

"I was in army. It was . . . *beeez-neees treep.*"

*

I need to listen to more jazz
Because jazz is where it's at
And you need to listen to more jazz
Because I want to be a cool cat
And a cool cat I could be
With a pretty girl like you dancing with me
A cool cat you could say is twirling me around and he don't care what they say

We need to listen to more jazz
Because jazz is like we two
Most folks don't understand it
But we know just what to do
Oh they say it's just some complicated song

But half the fun is to make it up as you go along

-    Vladimir, 2002

Jazz was a constant presence in my life during Peace Corps, even though I was hardly the connoisseur I thought I was at the time. I have several vivid memories with various jazz records as a soundtrack. I was really into Sun Ra's *Space is the Place* record, particularly when I was in Vladimir. I remember acquiring two pivotal Mingus records while in Russia. I ordered a copy of *The Black Saint and the Sinner Lady* from Amazon, which my parents brought to me when they visited. And there was a copy of *Mingus Ah Um* for sale in a tiny electronics shop that Chris and I had stumbled upon in Ekaterinburg. I remember it was really expensive, so much so that I initially didn't buy it until Christmas, as a gift to myself. The chaos and polyphony of these records seemed appropriate to the time and place, the multifaceted zeitgeist of Russia in the early 2000s.

Jazz was also a code, a language that Chris and I shared. I don't think either of us really knew much about jazz at the time, but we both wanted to and we both pretended we did. It was a shared experience and interest for the two of us that was exclusive to our friendship, part of the aspirational posturing both of us were undergoing in our early 20s.

This pose became comical when it encountered reality. When we were at the reception at Spaso House the night before we all left, the U.S. Ambassador dropped into the party for a while. I remember Chris and I found ourselves talking to him, and somehow it came out that he was also a fan of Charles Mingus. Chris and I, both of us having had too much to drink by this point, started peppering him with the only three Mingus records we knew, "*Black Saint* this" and "*Ah Um* that" and "Isn't 'Better Get Hit In Your Soul,'" - probably the most well-known Mingus song - "great?", convinced that because we knew these records and thought they were the best, this had to be a universal opinion, rather than just clichés spouted by two kids who didn't know any better. The Ambassador floored us by letting us know that he had something on the order of twenty Charlie Mingus records and that his favorite was *Tijuana Moods*, which neither Chris nor I had ever heard of. It was a checkmate move if there ever was one. He graciously offered to have his picture taken with us before slinking away.

These verses were never set to music, and I never had any intention of doing so. I wrote them with Liz in mind. I wanted to capture the exuberance of the early stages of our relationship. I find it interesting that I was all but admitting that liking jazz was a step that one has to take to be "cool." There was a person I wanted to become, and that was a person who liked jazz. So much of my writing from this period betrays an insecurity that I wasn't smart enough, or cultured enough, or well-read enough. This wasn't a new impulse, for this insecurity and reactive posturing dated back to high school, when I stole a copy of *On the Road* from my friend's mom's bookshelf and decided one day that I liked jazz, despite not really knowing what jazz was. The absurdity of all this lay in the fact that I didn't bother to finish *On the Road* until years later and the jazz I listened to at first could charitably be described as shitty elevator music. The window dressing was enough.

I'd matured and developed a bit by the time I got to Russia, but the pose was still there, demanding that I work my way through thick Russian novels and listen to squeaky Sun Ra records and make pretentious wisecracks to my friends about both of those things, hoping they hadn't read *that* book or listened to *that* record and call me out.

But I think all of us were stretching and exploring at that time. Why else would we have bothered to go otherwise?

*

Interlude: As My Name's Shipuchin!, or Некультурность

I remember falling asleep at a production of *Chaika* in Vladimir with my American girlfriend.

*

You've been distant
Since you joined the Resistance
You headed for the hills
And don't come out on Friday night anymore

It's so boring
It's the same old story
'bout a girl who could commit murder
But she can't commit to me

Since you joined the Party
I've been lower than Trotsky

You traded all your records
For a job within the Cheka
And your favorite revolver
Ain't the one it used to be

It's so boring
It's the same old story
'bout a girl who could commit treason
But she can't commit to me

Since you joined the Party
I've been lower than Trotsky

-        Vladimir, 2002

I read a lot of books while in the Peace Corps. There was certainly enough time for it. When it was cold and dark and frozen outside, staying in and drinking something hot and/or alcoholic while reading a novel seemed to be the only reasonable thing to do. In the winter of 2002, I read *For Whom the Bell Tolls*, and it inspired this song. This was always a favorite to play at Peace Corps gatherings. Simon loved this song, and it's among my favorites too. I remember thinking the Trotsky line was a joke that I threw in intending to change, but I can't imagine the song without it. I remember being impressed with the double meaning of "commit." It seemed sophisticated. I'm sure the image of someone going off into the hills to fight with a bunch of militants had to be influenced by the news from Afghanistan. I remember reading articles in *Newsweek* about the various commanders in the Northern Alliance, portraits that made them seem like characters in an action movie, and of course talk of the mujahideen and al-Qaeda, to say nothing of Chechnya, was everywhere. The part about trading *Revolver* for an actual revolver and how that mystifies the protagonist was very much drawn from that era. So many of the people who organized and carried out the 9/11 attacks seemed "normal," and I struggled with how they could be driven to abandon "normality" in order to devote themselves to a violent cause.

Lyrically I think both this song and the next were influenced by two tracks from *69 Love Songs*, which I was listening to a lot at the time: "World Love" and "Abigail, Belle of Kilronan." Both had lyrics about going to war and a superficial romanticization of "revolution" that was accompanied by love, music, and wine. These were treated as lyrical devices, and I started using such tropes as backdrops for several of my songs. Neither of those songs had really struck me in the couple of years I had been listening to that record, but I remember noticing them and playing them deliberately that first fall in Russia. I'm sure that they permeated the imagery and tone of these.

*

I didn't want you to leave
Though I know that this ain't Texas
Someday we're going to sail to Tangier
And take life a little reckless

We could join the fleet or
We could ride the rails, yeah,

We could bed some girls
And make up more detail

I didn't want you to leave
Though I know that this ain't Paris
Someday we're going to land in Madrid
And, yeah, if they dare us

We could join the war or
We could kill the Tsar, yeah,
We could take this Revolution way too far
We could take this Revolution way too far
We could take this Revolution way too far
Yeah yeah yeah
We could take this Revolution way too far

-        Vladimir 2002

This one was also very much influenced by *For Whom the Bell Tolls* and Hemingway in general. There's also a bit of Beat Generation romanticism in it too. I read a lot of Kerouac while in Russia. When I wrote this, I had recently finished *Desolation Angels* and had a copy of *Big Sur* that I bought in Moscow.

I was driven to read Hemingway for a couple of reasons. I had a friend from my time in St. Petersburg named Heath. Heath was older, and seemed so much more worldly. He loved Hemingway, especially *For Whom the Bell Tolls*, and he suggested I read it, a recommendation I filed away for later.

What probably drove me to act on it was Mike, who was inevitably given the clichéd moniker "Texas Mike" to distinguish him from another Mike in our group, who also got geographically tagged as "L.A. Mike." I connected with Mike deeply. He was outgoing and audacious. He had a charisma and a coolness I found captivating. He seemed so alive. He was good looking and smart and humble and well read. I imagined him as some sort of Dean Moriarty to my Sal Paradise. I think I looked at Mike the way I looked at Heath; there was a symmetry, or slant rhyme between them.

I remember talking with Mike about writing during Training, and he told me he loved Hemingway. He quoted to me a line from *A Movable Feast* about writing simple, declarative sentences, which I wrote down and filed away in a book somewhere. No doubt this was on my mind as I bought *For Whom the Bell Tolls* at Angliya in Moscow before heading out to the provinces

The first line of this song refers to Mike's departure from Russia. He didn't last long. He was among the early casualties. Our group seemed pretty durable at first. There were fifty-six of us, and just about all of us made it through Training. The Peace Corps folks told us this was a rarity, but leaving early seemed so ridiculous, so unthinkable. I couldn't imagine why anybody who had gone through so much preparation, mental or otherwise, could give up so quickly. September 11th seemed to strengthen our collective resolve. To use a phrase that hadn't yet become laden with baggage, leaving then seemed to be letting the terrorists win. I saw myself and the Peace Corps as on the front line, and that the human connections and trust that we were building by our presence - especially among our former "enemy" - was what was going to lead us to a better world. I had never felt so naively idealistic.

But the Chekists that were then solidifying their power in the Russian government viewed us a being on the front line too, as agents of a Pax Americana that was infiltrating their country. We didn't know it at first but the campaign to oust us had begun before we even arrived.

I don't know the details of Mike leaving. I remember getting word that he had some run-ins with the FSB. I also remember hearing that there were some family problems at home. Either way, suddenly, he was gone. I wrote this song soon after, as I fantasized about us having further adventures together. I was sure it was going to happen. But I haven't been in touch with him since.

The other character in this was a Volunteer named Jen. I didn't know her well at all, but I liked her a lot. She had come into the Peace Corps having lived in Paris, thus the reference. She left even before Mike, not for any nefarious reason - she just packed it in. Russia is a lot of things, but if your point of reference is Paris, it's not going to match up.

Jen and Mike were among the first to leave but they certainly weren't the last. Each week that first winter seemed to bring news of someone else who had bailed, harassed by the KGB or because they were homesick, or whatever. I can't speak for anyone else but each casualty made me more determined to stay no matter what - I was going to be the last one standing. I never gave serious thought to leaving, despite some flirtation with the idea the second winter in Ekaterinburg, when lonely despair colored all aspects of my life. But even then, I didn't allow myself to take the mental exercise too far. Memories of that initial resolve carried a lot of weight. I remember conversations after various comrades had gone home. There was a bit of patronizing judgment. "Well, I guess they couldn't hack it." As much as anything else, this perceived social pressure was a governor limiting the extent of my consideration. I guess it's not that big of a deal, but I've always had a satisfaction being in the small group - nineteen - that made it all the way, even if a big chunk of the people who left were kicked out after the first year and had no choice in the matter.

*

Interlude: The New Russians, or Зенит

I remember meeting Maksim for the first time in a bar on Gagarina, eating peanuts and drinking beer. I remember playing soccer with him and his friends at the gym near the university. I remember scoring a goal and feeling respected. I remember playing goalie with such abandon that Maksim called me crazy.

*

Maksim was crazy.

Maksim was the son of a childhood friend of Valeri, one of the Russian instructors in Training. Soon after my arrival in Vladimir, Valeri arranged for us to meet. Maksim and I drank beer at a cafe on Gagarina. He had gone to college in St. Petersburg, we were both about the same age, we both liked music. I guess we hit it off.

Maksim's dad was wealthy. I don't know what he did, but I privately referred to him by that denigrating moniker "New Russian" - at the time a caricature of the *nouveau riche*, maybe - *probably* - corrupt, that was the butt of jokes in Russia circles in the 1990s. One of these jokes went:

A New Russian is approached by a friend as he parks his new Mercedes.
"Didn't you just buy a Mercedes last week?" the friend asks.
"I did," replies the New Russian.
"Well why did you buy another one?"
"The ashtray was full."

Maksim lived in a detached house off Gagarina, not far from the Assumption Cathedral. I couldn't tell you exactly where it was because I never went there on foot. Maksim would always pick me up. He drove a late model Lada, but this was clearly a starter car. His dad drove a Nissan Maxima, which Maksim coveted, in part because "Nissan Maxima" means "Maksim's Nissan" in Russian.

He was a car guy. In addition to the Nissan, Maksim loved the UAZ, the beefy Rrrrrrrussian Dzheep. "*Ooooaaazzz, Rrrrrrrussian Dzheep,*" he'd say. His dad apparently had had one of these Rrrrrrrussian Dzheeps at one point. Maksim used to tell a story about how his dad wanted to prove the superiority of the UAZ to the American original by driving his UAZ across the Klyazma River - not across a bridge, but *across the river,* bank to bank. What prompted this particular maximalist fit of auto nationalism I never knew, but it was apparently strong enough that his dad was prepared to sacrifice the

Rrrrrrrussian Dzheep, and quite possibly his life, to prove the worth of the UAZ, for although the Klyazma isn't exactly the Mississippi, it's more than a creek.

I imagined as if the entire city gathered along the banks to watch his dad, some provincial Russian Evel Knievel, do the impossible, proving his own moxie while sticking it to the Americans. It seemed like a short story: a festival-like atmosphere, the citizens of Vladimir waiting, hoping, fearing, as he drives into the rush of the river, that heart-stopping moment when, as he approaches the midpoint, the water tops the roof of the Rrrrrrrussian Dzheep, but, critically, doesn't overtake the exhaust pipe, which peeks like a periscope above the waterline to assure the spectators that all was well. He emerges on the other side to cheers, Party officials handing out medals, a feast day declared.

The actual denouement of this story was never clear to me. He may or may not have made it.

I met his dad a couple of times.

I never once saw the UAZ.

Maybe the ashtray was full.

*

Interlude: New Slang

After hanging out a few times, Maksim told me that my Russian needed to be slangified, so he taught me a few phrases. One was «Колбасимся!» which he said means "Let's party!" Another was «Давай зажигаем!» which he said means "Let's party!"

*

Maksim would show up at my place unannounced. There'd be a knock on my door, I'd open it and see Maksim, and that would be it. That would be the evening.

"*Dooglas, we will take two beers...*"

Sometimes we would take two beers and wind up playing soccer with some of his buddies. Sometimes we would take two beers and wind up at his dacha in Suzdal, drinking cognac in the snow. Sometimes we would take two beers and wind up at his house, playing guitars and piano and drinking *samogon*. Or *yorsh*.

It was fun, but it became too much.

"*Dooglas, we will take two beers...*"

After a while, I began to have a sense of dread when there was an unexpected knock on my door. I found myself avoiding my place at nights I thought were likely he'd stop by. Maksim was nothing but nice to me, but it was too intense. I couldn't do it anymore. It was the first time in my life I stopped hanging out with someone because they exhausted me.

Eventually he got the hint.

On my last night in Russia, at Spaso House, Valeri approached me and asked if I wanted him to pass on a message to Maksim. I thought for a minute. The best I could come up with was, "Tell him I said hi. And I'm sorry."

*

Interlude: Podmoskovnye Vechera

A perk of living in Vladimir was its proximity to Moscow. It was easy to take the train into the city for the day and I did so quite often, just to get away for a bit. I almost always went by myself. It was terrific.

My usual routine when I went to Moscow from Vladimir was to take the Metro to Okhotny Ryad, walk around Red Square, and then walk up Tverskaya to the McDonald's off of Pushkinskaya, and then walk down Tverskoi Bulvar to Angliya to buy a book or two. One day in the summer of 2002 I went up to Hotel Kosmos and then bummed around VDNKh, which I had not seen since 1991.

I loved wandering around Moscow by myself. It made me fall in love with that city.

*

The worst part about death - the worst part! - is that there will be a last time I listen to this record. And honey - that's not fair.

- Vladimir, 2002

I scribbled this into my notebook while sitting on my bed in my room. I was spending the day at home, alone, reading, listening to records, drinking coffee, playing guitar, writing.

It was a perfect day.

I remember the record I was referring to, but I think I'll keep it with mine. To this day, every time I listen to it - which is often - it feels like a victory over death.

*

For all the memories I have of that first year in Russia, so many of my favorites are those from when I was alone. Alone in my room in Vladimir, reading, listening to records, drinking coffee, playing guitar, writing. Alone at Tamara and Valentin's apartment, doing much of the same. Alone, wandering the streets of Moscow, and Vladimir, or taking the long way to our training sessions in Zelenograd.

I needed these opportunities for disengagement, to pull back from the intensity of being who I was, where I was, when I was there. When I was alone, I didn't have to be The American, or The Volunteer. I didn't have to engage with the world that had revealed itself to be more complex and scarier than I had naively imagined it to be in the pre-9/11 '90s of my youth. I didn't have to cycle through grammatical conjugations in my brain to accomplish mundane tasks like buying a loaf of bread.

I could just be alone.

But I wasn't lonely.

That came later.

*

If spending a day by myself, disengaged from the world, was a coping mechanism for all of the intensity of my life in Russia, the other method was to go see Melanie.

I was really lucky to have Melanie in Vladimir with me. I wondered about a lot of things in the months leading up to Peace Corps, but one thing I never considered was another Volunteer at site with me. Had I done so, I scarcely could have imagined that I'd go through such an intense experience with someone so ideal, someone whose temperament was so well matched to my own.

Melanie and I did a lot together. We'd meet each other for pizza downtown until the proprietors yelled at us for some reason, after which we switched to a Middle Eastern place on Bolshaya Moskovskaya. Whenever I wrote a new song, I'd go over to her *obschezhitiye* to play it for her. We went on a trip to St. Petersburg together in the spring. It's not like it was every day, or even every week, but we never went very long without seeing each other. For all of the various characters that came in and out of my life while in Vladimir, she was the constant, the center of gravity that I needed to keep a chaotic year of my life in order.

No matter what happened to me in Russia, I knew that as long as Melanie was around, I'd be fine.

*

Interlude: Customer Relations

I remember buying a CD player at the department store in Vladimir soon after I arrived. The door was broken when I took it out of the box. I returned it to the store. The clerk blamed me. If I placed a heavy book on top to weigh it down, it worked fine. I used my Russian-English dictionary and a Daniil Kharms anthology.

*

Me and Jane
We don't talk too much no more
She don't need a guy
Who don't know the score
She's like the tea that I drink
She's from Long Island
And stronger than you think

Me and Jane
We're not among the lucky few
Don't send us an invitation
You better send us two
I said things that I knew would hurt
And acceptance of this is simply a just dessert
Me and Jane

Me and Jane
We've had our fair share of frustration
Since I got caught
Chasing a girl's persuasion
She told me there's not much left to say
I'd done all the talking
And it was going to stay that way

Me and Jane
We've not a lot left to do
She found an apartment
And I found one too
We'll have a fight or two about some books
But I won't sacrifice a novel

To get off the hook
Me and Jane

-        Vladimir, 2002

I spent a fair amount of the spring and summer of 2002 listening to Bruce Springsteen, especially songs from *The Ghost of Tom Joad* and *Nebraska*. I had always been a fan, but I was especially drawn to him during this time. I enjoyed the characters that he wrote about, how it seemed as if certain personalities stretched across songs, almost like a biography. And they all had names. I started doodling in my notebook about Jane. I don't know why I selected that name. Probably it just seemed like a normal name. It didn't evoke anything. It didn't stand out. One of my students was named Zhenya, and her "English name" was Jane, but I don't think I was thinking about her at all. I remember at one point in my musings, Jane moved to Pittsburgh after "taking classes." It was very Bruce. Eventually her story evolved into a breakup song after my relationship with Liz ended.

There are parts of this song that I really like. The line about Jane being from Long Island always made me chuckle, but I wonder if it's a bit too clever. I like the line "chasing a girl's persuasion," which originally had been in a much earlier song I had written before Russia. I like how that verse concludes with Jane telling the protagonist to not even bother trying to explain things, which leads to him becoming really petty in the final verse. It was probably his natural inclination anyway. That Jane delivers this retort in response to his suggestion that she just has to get over what he did is a nice reassertion of power in the dynamic.

*

Interlude: Your Mother Should Know

I remember my mother sending a letter to Melanie thanking her for being my friend. Upon receiving it, Melanie laughed for twenty minutes straight.

*

My name's not important
My mom called me dear, my dad called me son
My girl called me the one

It started out easy
It started as weeks and turned into months
It was a lot of fun

And I had to leave her
Not 'cause I'm mean and not 'cause I'm cruel
Because I was a fool

On the inside lane my car it did run
'Cause you're tempted to hug
what you're pulled away from

I wrote her a letter
Said I found a job and I found someone

Said I found a reason

I didn't send it
I lit a match and I opened the flue
'Cause it, it's not true

So I drove to Philly
I'd meet some friends and we'd have a bash
Then I had that crash

On the inside lane my car it did run
'Cause you're tempted to hug
What you're pulled away from

-        Vladimir, 2002

This was written around the same time as "Me and Jane," two breakup songs, twinned. It's also very Bruce, an attempt to write a song for *Nebraska*. It's two chords, rhythmic, with a flat melody. Over the years it's gotten more dissonant. As far as my songs go, I like it a lot.

Hijazi always seemed to like these songs. Hijazi was Melanie's boyfriend for most of the winter of 2002. He was from Syria. He was tall and had monstrous hands. Once, he picked up a guitar, and I tried to show him how to play a chord, but his massive fingers couldn't fit on the frets.

Shortly after I wrote these songs, he invited me over with a weird sense of urgency. When I got to the *obschezhitiye*, he handed me Melanie's guitar, pulled out a camcorder, and told me to play them. I have no idea why he wanted to film me playing these songs, or any others, but he was insistent. I said ok. I sat on the window sill and belted them out, as he zoomed in and out and moved around the room.

Hijazi was often like that. Insistent. He was insistent that I come over for dinner. He was insistent that he cut my hair when it got shaggy. He was insistent that I stay just a little longer when I was begging off to go home. Insistent.

I'm not sure I ever knew exactly what Hijazi was doing in Vladimir. I think he had some sort of business connection, but I don't know. He was one of several Arabs living in Melanie's *obschezhitiye*, and easily the most sociable. He was constantly talking, in English, in Russian, in Arabic, punctuating his speech with a huge smile and long draws on his L&M cigarettes.

He and I became pretty close that spring. By then, Liz and I had broken up, which cut me off from the social circle of the American Home. Hijazi's relationship with Melanie had gotten complicated - when I went over to play for his camcorder, he was with a tall Russian girl he insisted he wasn't sleeping with, but I didn't believe him. He and I would meet up downtown and drink beer on top of the old city walls, or watch soccer in the *obschezhitiye*. He introduced me into a community of foreign students lodging at the university. They were from all over the Middle East, as well as West Africa and elsewhere. For all of the effortless intermingling I did between two worlds - Russian and American - here was the proverbial Third World, though instead of a competition for its loyalty, both America and Russia seemed to treat it with disdain.

It's hard to talk about it without unfairly reducing him to a proxy for his ethnicity and religion, but I was glad to meet Hijazi when I did. The media - Russian and American

- were bombarding the world with images of scary Muslim men. Osama bin Laden was twinned with the mysterious Ibn al-Khattab, the supposed mastermind, along with Shamil Basaev, of the string of apartment bombings across Russia in 1999, while I was a student in St. Petersburg. The second war in Chechnya dragged on. Anyone with a dark complexion was likely to be stopped by the *Militsiya* and asked for documents, if not a bribe, profiling I wasn't subjected to due to my fair skin and European features. As long as I didn't open my mouth, it was easy for me to pass as a Russian.

Indeed, I was welcomed, not because I was an American, but because I was a "Slavic brother," which I got a lot when people learned my last name. This had some perks, but it also meant that I was privy to some comments that may have in other circumstances been more discreet. I remember telling someone I knew in Vladimir that I had recently tried kharcho, a kind of soup from the Caucasus. «Террористический суп» - "terrorist soup" - she spat. There was open disdain for Vladimir's small Roma population. Though physical violence was rare, the contempt and hostility were overt. I'm ashamed that I internalized the bigotry, heeding advice to hurry past when one would approach me on the sidewalk, the constant warnings that they were going to pick my pocket if I wasn't careful activating the flight mechanism in my brain. Reading the news about hostility towards Arabs and Muslims back home in the wake of September 11th reinforced that America and Russia are slant rhymes of each other. Russia was in the process of reimagining itself, replacing Marxism-Leninism with a retread of Orthodoxy, Autocracy, and Nationality. America was proclaiming itself as a defender of a narrowly defined "freedom," wielded like a club against a heretic Other, or perhaps, I feared, embracing the enlightened bigotry of a character like Pim Fortuyn.

I don't know the extent to which Hijazi was subjected to this nonsense. He never let on. And of course, he wasn't perfect either. He insisted on a number of occasions that the Mossad was behind September 11th as part of a Jewish conspiracy to get the world to hate Muslims. That he said this while dating Melanie, who is Jewish, demonstrated the complexity of it all. Or the absurdity. Apart from the stray comment, we didn't talk about it much. Our friendship was either bigger or smaller than that.

The last time I saw Hijazi, he and I were riding in a *marshrutka* together. At the corner of Gagarina and Bolshaya Moskovskaya, Hijazi got out. I was about to go meet my parents in St. Petersburg, and, although I didn't know yet that I was going to move to Ekaterinburg, we knew there was some uncertainty ahead. I can see Hijazi smiling and waving, the 900-year-old gold cupolas topped with Orthodox crosses of the Assumption Cathedral peeking above the trees, serving as a backdrop.

"Don't worry. We'll see each other again," he said.

He was insistent.

*

Interlude: The Clash of Civilizations

I remember watching the World Cup with Hijazi and a bunch of his friends in the *obschezhitiye* that Melanie lived in. Later we organized a table tennis tournament. The USA finished in last place.

*

She quit me like she quit smoking
She only calls me when she's drunk
She's been down since she up and did it
She won't admit it but I know she's in a funk

So raise a glass tonight and toast to Scandinavian skies
It should come as no surprise that the drinks are on me
So raise a glass tonight and toast to Scandinavian skies
It should come as no surprise that she's a bit tipsy

She reminds me a lot of Boston Harbor
She's a little dirty and she's got a taste for tea
I'd throw her out if I had a backbone
Instead I had a sidecar and you know what that does to me

So raise a glass tonight and toast to Scandinavian skies
It should come as no surprise that the drinks are on me
So raise a glass tonight and toast to Scandinavian skies
It should come as no surprise that she's a bit tipsy

-       Vladimir, 2002

This is one of the few songs I wrote in Russia that is completely divorced from that context. I remember writing it at the desk in my room in Vladimir but I could have written this anywhere, devoid as it is of any references or observations or connections to where I was living at the time. It seemed like a small triumph when I wrote it but I have very little attachment to it now. I don't think I wrote it about anything or anyone in particular. I wrote it sometime in the spring, after Liz and I broke up, but I'm certain it doesn't have anything to do with that. It's on the whole too clever. It has a Stephin Merritt vibe to it, which would make sense, as I was listening to a lot of his records at the time. I recycled the line about Boston Harbor from something I wrote in college. I wrote the line about the sidecar after reading the liner notes of *69 Love Songs* in which Stephin Merritt mentions it as a drink he enjoys. I had no idea what's in a sidecar. Shortly after coming back home, I was in Panama City, Florida with Melanie and Simon and Laura and Adam and Rob and Andrew and I ordered one at a restaurant and the server joked that it was an "old lady's drink." I learned later that "Scandinavian Skies" is also the title of a song by Billy Joel.

Everything about this one is weird.

*

Interlude: Phone My Family Tell Them I'm Lost on the Sidewalk

I listened to *Yankee Hotel Foxtrot* as I walked around town in the spring of 2002. I listened to "I Am Trying to Break

Your Heart" and its drum fills as I walked between the garages out past Zarya to Prospekt Lenina. I listened to "Jesus, Etc." as I walked downtown on roads parallel to Bolshaya Moskovskaya.

***

На Байкале

Interlude: Siberia, Siberia

I remember Melanie reading me excerpts from *Infinite Jest* as we lurched across the continent going to Baikal. I remember reading *Everything is Illuminated* on the ride back (having finished *Crime and Punishment* and *The Foundation Pit* on the lake).

*

There's a bar in St. Petersburg I used to go to when I was studying there called Fish Fabrique. It was pretty divey, with tiny booths and cheap Russian beer, and they would project art films on the walls. It was cool. Towards the end of the semester, I went there with a bunch of expat friends. We had a fun night. We were all pretty smitten with the intoxicating, privileged life you could live at the time as a Westerner in Russia. Many of us were already making at least mental plans to return, somehow, someway. At a certain point, the stereo in the bar started blasting "No Sleep Till Brooklyn." One of us ad libbed "No Sleep Till Vladivostok!" and soon we all were parading around the cramped bar mimicking the trains plodding across the continent towards the Pacific, some 5,000 miles away. That night, out on Ligovsky Prospekt, as we stumbled into cabs to take us back to our *obschezhitiye* on Vasilievsky Island, we motioned across the street towards Moskovsky Vokzal, the main train station in the city, and the start of the Trans-

Siberian, and made boastful plans, that one day, we'd ride the train east, out into Siberia.

It was a neat fantasy that I promptly forgot about. I wanted to return to Russia, but my orientation was decidedly western. As I plotted my return over the next year and a half, it was with thoughts of going back to St. Petersburg, or maybe Moscow.

Definitely not Vladimir.

Siberia never crossed my mind.

*

Interlude: How Far Are You Willing to Go to Make A Difference?

I told Peace Corps that the idea of living in Siberia was "overwhelming" because I was afraid my dad was going to die while I was overseas.

*

When our teaching responsibilities ended for the summer, Peace Corps expected us to find some sort of work to do. Usually this meant teaching at a summer camp or someplace similar. We were encouraged to stay somewhat close to our site, though this wasn't vigorously enforced. Still, there was enough of a hold on me to limit the radius of my search. Peace Corps framed the geographical limitations with the idea of committing to your site and your region, that you'd further demonstrate your dedication to embedding yourself into the community by staying in the area year-round, rather than traipsing off to some other place. This made enough sense to me. I bought into it. I talked with Polina about a couple of opportunities in Vladimirskaya Oblast', and was looking into a summer camp near Ryazan, about a hundred miles to the southwest. Eventually I decided to work at a camp on Lake Baikal in Eastern Siberia.

Baikal was 2,500 miles away.

Close enough.

It was Melanie's idea to go to Baikal, and it was a good one. If going to Siberia was an abstraction, going to Baikal was like going to the moon. It would require a five-day train ride just to get to Irkutsk, some 500 miles beyond Krasnoyarsk, the furthest east where there were Volunteers. It was practically off the map.

Baikal itself is shrouded in legend. The world's oldest lake, and the deepest, it occupies a mythical place in the Russian psyche. The Siberian writer Valentin Rasputin, who led efforts in Soviet times to block industrial development that threatened the unique ecology of the lake, writes:

> When people encountered Baikal a song would begin to sound forth of its own accord: words would form, derived from the mysterious depths of the origin and behavior of "the glorious sea" and, accompanied by the noise of the wind, the lapping waves, and the view all around, would be continually strung together until they formed, like a new tributary, an exhalation of gratitude.

Seeing Baikal was likened to being born again. I had never considered the idea of standing on its shores, but once I did, I knew I had to go.

Поехали.

*

We left Vladimir late at night. Melanie and I hung out with Hijazi at a cafe on Bolshaya Moskovskaya in the hours leading up to our departure. The train, traveling between Moscow and Irkutsk, slid into the station. We climbed aboard, found our berths, and we were off. I was excited, but fell asleep almost immediately.

When I awoke, we were approaching Nizhny Novgorod, which at the time served as my own personal frontier. I had visited the city a few months before, and it was the farthest east I had ever been. The train clacked across the bridge spanning the Volga. From that point on, every minute, every second, every kilometer was a new record for me. It was exhilarating! For the next three days that we were on that train, I had this weird rush pulsing through my veins. It was all uncharted territory, the train burrowing ever further into the expanse of the east. I was never bored on that absurdly long ride. How could I be? I felt like Sal Paradise, poring over the maps in my copy of *Lonely Planet*, tracing the path of the train the way he drew "one long red line called Route 6 . . . clear to Ely, Nevada, and . . . down to Los Angeles." My own route would be punctuated by places with names like Kirov and Perm', the train barreling towards the Ural Mountains, across the continental divide, and into Asia, into Siberia.

After we crossed the Volga, the next landmark of note was the dividing line between Europe and Asia. There's an obelisk along the tracks about thirty-five kilometers west of Ekaterinburg. I figured we'd get there late at night, and I promised myself I'd be awake for it. Time is a bit of an abstraction on a train ride as long as this one. The clocks on the train are set to Moscow Time but it's a useless reference. Your body's Circadian rhythm is thrown off after the first day, and you enter this weird suspended animation. Everyone is affected a little differently. The people around you on the train all sleep and eat at different intervals, making their own peace with the warped time.

The sun went down and my body began to tire. I climbed into my berth and gazed out the window, the posts along the line and the steady percussion of the tracks making the world sliding by feel like a chronophotographic movie, frame by frame by frame, occasionally scrambled by a train moving in the other direction.

My eyelids began to droop. I knew we were getting close. I forced them open, trying to make out the kilometer markers on the side. Is that it? Is that the obelisk or just an anonymous post on the side of the tracks? I began to drift into sleep. No, I have to stay awake. The train let out a whistle, my head fell to the pillow, that's it, that has to be it, that was the obelisk, right, maybe I can stay awake until we get to Ekaterinburg, I've always wanted to go there, I wonder if I'll ever get there, just let me get a glimpse.

What continent am I on?

*

When I woke up, we were approaching Omsk. The train stopped for about a half hour, so we got off, and walked up and down the platform to stretch our legs. It was sunny, the big blue expanse of sky hanging over the blueish-green train station, which was ornamented in white trim and reminded me of a circus big top. Our *gopnik* carmates, decked out in track suits and Adidas sandals, milled about, smoking cigarettes. A collection of *babushki* lined up along the platform, selling salted fish, packages of noodles in a cup, plastic bottles of gin and tonic. I found myself staring at the station name: Omsk. Omsk! This was it. Not only Asia, but Siberia.

The next few days passed, measured not in hours, but in stops. Novosibirsk that night. Then Krasnoyarsk the next day, crossing the Yenesei on an iron truss bridge, past where our friends Andrew and Rob and Simon lived, the most distant Peace Corps outpost. Melanie had traveled to Krasnoyarsk the previous winter to visit. Now both of us were in uncharted territory.

We went through places called Taishet, and Nizhneudinsk, and a town called, appropriately, Zima, which means "winter." The expanses of the taiga were monotonous, but I never grew tired of gazing out the window. Melanie and I read books, and played *Durak*, and took naps, warmed up our instant noodles from the samovar down the corridor, and drank beer in the evenings. It wasn't boring. How could it be? Soon we would be in Irkutsk, and then at Baikal, but for now, we were lurching ever eastwards, deeper and deeper into Siberia

*

Interlude: Stop That Train, I'm Leaving

I remember getting terrible Chinese food in Irkutsk with Melanie upon arrival. I remember when our train arrived, nobody was there to meet us, as we had been expecting per email exchanges. I remember worrying that we had traveled 3,000 miles for nothing.

*

The director of the camp was named Sergei. Had he been born on the other side of the world, he would've been the type to thru-hike the Appalachian Trail or climb Denali while on break from a fancy college. As he was from Irkutsk, he spent his endless energy traversing the wilds around Baikal. In addition to running the camp, he led expeditions on foot and horseback that circumnavigated the lake. I had it in my mind that participants on these journeys were supposed to subsist on a few grams of salted fish and mushrooms gathered from the forest, but they were probably pretty posh.

When our train arrived, we were expecting him to meet us, but he wasn't there and I started imaging all of these absurd scenarios of being marooned in Irkutsk. He was apologetic when Melanie called him, and before too long he was bounding through the station to meet us. We loaded our stuff into his car, a Japanese sedan with a right-hand drive, like lots of cars in Irkutsk. I sat in the front seat, on the left, as he weaved in and out of traffic on his way back to his apartment.

The apartment was nice, spacious, with high ceilings and what would've been called in Russia "Евро-Ремонт" - "Euro renovations" - a name given to somewhat gaudy fixtures and modern domestic tech that wouldn't have been out of place in an American McMansion. His mother was there when we arrived. Melanie and I bummed around Irkutsk for the rest of the afternoon before heading to the camp the next day.

*

Sergei rode with us out to Baikal but didn't stay. He was represented at the camp by his wife, who wore a tiny bikini the entirety of the session, no matter how cold it got, and Andrei the Woodsman, who was an old friend.

The camp was on the eastern shore of Baikal, north of where the Selenga River flows into the lake. It was a small patch of clearing that emerged from the trees, mostly hearty evergreens that hugged the shore. There were a dozen tents scattered in groups of two or three on the edges of the clearing, and a covered common area where we ate our meals. A small shelter stood on the periphery that functioned as a shower of sorts. There was supposed to be a *banya*, but, unfortunately, that turned out to be a case of false advertising. Small waves lapped at a sandy beach. You could look across the lake and barely see the other side, about twenty-five miles away. Occasionally a herd of cows would wander through.

There were a few permanent staff, most of whom worked in the kitchen. Andrei the Woodsman took care of just about everything else. Andrei was always building something, hacking away at tree limbs to fashion whatever needed to be fashioned: a bench, a platform, a table. He was a fan of classic rock, and littered his conversations with references to his favorite songs. "*Dooglas,* look – a stairway . . . to heaven!" he said to me as he carried a ladder he had just built across the campground. Whenever he heard me playing guitar, he'd amble over and ask if I knew how to sing "House of the Rising Sun." When I reminded him that I couldn't remember the words, he'd reply with the same refrain.

"Too bad good song."

It was a pretty leisurely time. We taught a couple of classes a day, but there was plenty of opportunity to relax. We spent a lot of time hiking up and down the beach. There were lots of knotted ropes hanging from branches cantilevering over the water which were fun to swing on. No one seemed to give a thought to letting go of the rope to splash into the lake. I went swimming just about every day, but even in July the water probably wasn't any more than sixty degrees or so, and I could only take about ten minutes before I had to get out. I'd throw on a sweater and warm up by the fire, a near eternal flame Andrei the Woodsman tended to.

Soon after our arrival, we were taken down the beach to another site. It was a camp for young Buryats from Ulan Ude. The head of the camp, a Russian, had heard there were a number of Americans on the lake and invited us to meet his group. Since both our camp session and theirs were starting, he thought it appropriate to summon some sort of blessing from Baikal. Local tradition holds that Baikal is a sacred sea, and Buryat shamans have elaborate rituals to commune with the spirits who reside in the lake. I don't know how authentic this guy's sacraments were, but it was cool. Since everything in Russia demands a certain syncretism, he began by pouring vodka into a glass, which he held aloft as he asked for Baikal's blessing of our visit. He turned, addressing his audience of Buryat students and American teachers, worked himself up, his voice crescendoing, rising to a climax, after which he flung the contents of the glass towards the water's edge. A true sacrifice.

*

We were joined on the lake by two other Volunteers, Anya and Micah. Micah was an aspiring sports writer from Seattle who was always smiling. At early morning classes during Training, he was smiling. During tedious lectures about whatever, he was smiling. At social events, of course, he was smiling. It was pretty charming and sweet, though I'll admit I laughed when another Volunteer once commented, "I like Micah but sometimes I want to punch that goddamn smile off his face."

Anya got a bad rap. I knew Anya pretty well. She was from Rochester and had gone to college at the University of Delaware. We were in the same Russian class during Training. She and I had the most Russian experience of the group, and so we were selected to give the Volunteer remarks when we were sworn in at Spaso House before going out to site. Anya was smart and hardworking and dedicated and of course people gave her shit about that. I remember glancing around the conference room during Staging in D.C. the very first day and watching Anya *own* one of the ice breaker activities that so many of us dismissed as stupid bullshit. She was all in on the oversized paper on an easel, manically doing charades, and writing out Russian words, even though no one else except for me could read them. From the start, Anya did everything right, and I'm ashamed that at times I joined the gallery of eye rolls in response to her energy and drive.

Even though we had our own classes, we collaborated on a lot of lessons. I threw a few resources into my bag when packing, but I can't say I had a lot. Anya, of course, brought it, dispensing all manner of activities that could be differentiated for our classes. She had ideas, and adaptations, and could think on her feet. She was a really good teacher.

Teaching was great. Classes were loose and interactive. Recreation was at least as important as the classes, and it was hard not to have fun on the lake. At one point, Micah and I came across a couple of students, along with Andrei the Woodsman, using a hatchet to shave the sides of a tree branch. They told us they were carving a bat for *lapta*, an old Russian folk game that's a bit like cricket, but that they had messed up. "It's too narrow for *lapta*." Too narrow for *lapta*, maybe, but perfect for baseball. We didn't quite have enough space for a diamond, but we organized a competition to see who could hit a tennis ball the farthest, something of a home run derby on the eastern shore of Lake Baikal. The contest was called when someone launched the ball deep into the woods beyond the southern edge of the campsite. We retreated back to the fire, threw the bat into the flames, and Andrei the Woodsman asked me to sing "House of the Rising Sun."

"Too bad good song."

About the only activity that fell flat was when Anya, Micah, Melanie, and I decided to collaborate on a camp-wide scavenger hunt for all the students. We crowded into a tent the night before the lesson to plan. Having students with a variety of different abilities, we wanted to build in a few advantages for the younger kids whose English wasn't as good as some of the older ones. This was a noble idea. Unfortunately, we were having these discussions while working our way through a few bottles of wine that we had bought at the village down the beach earlier that day. I don't quite know what happened, but nothing went according to our plans. The high school aged kids returned to the camp with all of the items on the list within about fifteen minutes while the little kids mostly got lost in the woods.

It was a disaster.

*

One of the characters we met on the lake was the father of one of the students. I don't remember his name so I'll call him Sasha. Sasha came in his own ride, a white Japanese sedan. He followed the bus on the circuitous ten-hour ride from Irkutsk, around the southern tip of the lake, across the Selenga Delta, and to the camp itself.

It was a treacherous route, full of hairpin turns on narrow ribbons of road, parallel to the railroad. You could see why this was the last section of the Trans-Siberian they were able to build, the engineers threading the needle between the mountains and the water. As we turned north and drove up the eastern shore of the lake, the highway separated from the shore, the mountains receded, and we crossed the alluvial plain towards the Selenga. The bus turned off the main road once we hit the river, where we stopped to wait for the ferry to take us across. The highway continued on, turning east and then south, navigating the mountain passes that had been carved by the Selenga towards Ulan Ude. Looking across the river you could see three or four piers that had been constructed as part of an unfinished bridge spanning the channel where we were waiting. For whatever reason, the project had been abandoned, seemingly quite some time earlier, the piers standing naked, threads of rebar sprouting like hairs from the concrete.

Once we got to the campsite, Sasha parked in a grove of trees not far from the beach, but separated from the main part of the camp. He pitched his own tent near his car. Although he ate with the rest of us, he also had his own stock of provisions stored in the trunk of the sedan. I was unsure what, if any, role he had at the place. He wasn't serving in any obvious capacity. He certainly wasn't teaching any of the classes. His English was broken at best. He kept an eye on his daughter, but he wasn't an overbearing chaperone. I thought maybe he was a free agent, accompanying us on the trek and using our site as a base camp to do his own thing, but he was always there. He didn't go off fishing or hiking or anything else. He was just around, which, to be sure, was fine.

On the first day of the camp, we all wrote our names on slips of paper and put them in a hat. Everyone was to have a "secret friend" for the week. You were supposed to give your secret friend little gifts every day: a drawing, or a poem, maybe a chocolate bar or a bag of chips if you went into the village. There was a fair amount of subterfuge that was expected. You were supposed to keep your secret friend guessing your identity before the big reveal on the last day of the session. Since there weren't very many of us at the camp, this proved to be a somewhat challenging task, and there was a lot of strategizing about how to keep your secret friend off your trail, ruses developed, elaborate systems of delivery devised.

When it was my turn to draw a name, I drew Sasha.

Finding gifts for a middle-aged man was new to me, but I had a plan. Realizing that anything written, either in English or Russian, would give me away, I decided the only way to keep my anonymity was to rely on things I could buy at the store in the village. So that's what Sasha got: junk food. Still, I thought it would be fun to devise ways of covering my tracks, giving the candy or whatever to Melanie to give to Sergei's wife to give to Anya to give to Micah to give to Andrei the Woodsman to give to Sasha.

I was apparently good at this. Towards the end of the week, Sasha confessed to me that he was totally stumped as to who his secret friend was, and that this was frustrating him to no end. Most of us by that point had a pretty good idea of who was sending us gifts. The camp after all wasn't big, and people were starting to get lazy about it anyway. Mine, a preteen camper, gave herself away midweek when she signed her name in a note and told me she loved me. I took Sasha's admission as a sign to go in for the kill.

The next day, I decided, I would deliver his gift myself.

My final gift to him was a bit anticlimactic - a bag of Estrella chips flavored with dill - but it didn't matter. I was ready. That morning, as we were milling about, ready to begin our final day on the lake, I grabbed the chips from my tent and approached Sasha.

"This is from your secret friend."

He looked at me and frowned.

"*Dooglas, please,* you must tell me who is my secret friend."

"Sasha, I can't. I'm sorry."

"*Dooglas, please.* If you can't tell me, you can say if he is adult or kid?"

I figured this bit of information was fine to reveal.

"Ok Sasha. An adult."

"Be right back."

He turned and walked across the camp towards the grove of trees where he had parked his car. He rummaged around in the trunk for a bit before closing the door and walking back towards me.

"*Dooglas, please* - give this to my secret friend."

He handed me a half liter aluminum can. It was a can of beer.

Baltika 0.

Non-alcoholic.

I awkwardly mumbled something about how his secret friend would've preferred something with a bit more kick, but I don't think he understood me.

"Ok, Sasha, I will."

The next morning, when all the secret friends were revealed, he was surprised and laughed when he learned my identity. I gave an embarrassed smile and shrugged my shoulders. I held up the can and suggested we drink it then and there, together, but he declined.

"*Dooglas,* I have long drive ahead. No time for beer."

This didn't make much sense to me but I didn't argue. He got into his sedan and drove off. I never saw him again.

I kept the can of Baltika 0 for several months. It became pretty well-traveled. When I got back to Vladimir, I set it on my desk, next to my books, with other souvenirs from the trip. When it was time to leave Vladimir, I packed it and took it to Moscow. It then traveled with me back across the continent to Ekaterinburg, where it stood next to the bottle of vodka Adam gave to me when he left Russia.

Sometime that winter, on a whim, I decided to drink it. I poured some into a glass, made sure to give a little nod towards Irkutsk, towards Sasha, then I downed it.

It was awful.

*

Interlude: You Can't See Across Belgium

I remember the bus stopping on a mountain road somewhere near Baikalsk on the way back to Irkutsk. I remember listening to *Burrito Deluxe* on the trip.

*

On our return from Baikal, we spent one more night at Sergei's place before catching the train back to Vladimir. I remember drinking tea with his mother just before we left for the *vokzal*. Sergei was out somewhere and we were waiting for his return before our departure. His mother was older, and seemed a touch aristocratic. We were asking about their family name - Rasputin. It's not an uncommon name in Russia, but for many - myself included - it can't help but conjure up images of the mad monk of Revolutionary Petrograd. That silly Boney M. song blasted from the kitchen at the camp seemingly every day, as it did in many places around Russia, so the connection was fresh in my mind. I admitted as much to her, with no small amount of embarrassment. She was gracious, though she had probably heard it all before. No, there wasn't any connection between their family and the infamous figure from history. Her husband's family were natives of Irkutskaya Oblast', a good 1,500 miles from where *that Rasputin* originated.

"What did your husband do? Is he still alive?"

"Yes, he's a writer."

Just then, we heard the door to the apartment open. I could hear Sergei's voice, along with someone's I didn't recognize.

Sergei came into the kitchen and looked at Melanie and me.

"Ready to go?"

It was time for us to go to the *vokzal* to catch our train home. I got up to get my bag.

Standing in the corridor by the front door was Sergei's father, Valentin Grigoryevich.

Valentin Grigoryevich Rasputin.

Valentin Rasputin.

The Siberian writer.

*

The ride back to Vladimir was considerably less exciting, like falling back to earth after visiting the moon. The scenery that had been a source of wonder as we rolled east became monotonous and boring, and I felt claustrophobic inside our compartment. I spent most of the time reading, taking naps, occasionally visiting the dining car. I got a bit of a rush as we pulled into Ekaterinburg, this time arriving during the day. I looked out into the city, so different from Vladimir, with trams and wide boulevards. I wondered if I'd ever get to visit. A little while later, I glanced out the window to see the obelisk dividing Eurasia into two.

One day in the dining car we met an American who overheard our English. He had been traveling around Asia the previous month and was riding the train all the way across from Beijing to Moscow, from where he planned to fly home.

"I can't wait to get to Moscow."

"It's great. What do you want to see?"

"Lenin. I saw Mao and Ho. When I see Lenin, I'll have seen the whole trinity."

Ленин жил.

***

Russia-American Владимировец

Shortly after I returned from Baikal, my parents came to visit. I met them in St. Petersburg, at the Hotel Moskva, the afternoon they arrived. I got into town that morning, having ridden the train overnight from Vladimir. I spent the day wandering the streets of the city I had fallen in love with two and a half years before.

Just before I was to meet them, I went to get a bite to eat at The Idiot, an expat hangout I frequented when I was a student. It's a cool spot, tucked into an asymmetrical, angular space along the Moika. I went there for the nostalgia, but also because they would pour you a complimentary shot of vodka when you sat down at a table. I needed the courage. I was nervous to see my parents. Nervous to see them after a year. Nervous to see them in Russia. Nervous for Russia to see them. Nervous for them to see me. In Russia. It was a collision of worlds.

I didn't really know what my parents made of my decision to go to Russia. I hadn't demonstrated a lot of direction in college, but they had always been generous and patient, indulging my thoughts to study in St. Petersburg, and my move to Chapel Hill afterwards to play in a band. I'm sure their patience was running a little thin when I signed up for the Peace Corps. They were outwardly supportive, but I know my dad in particular was a little skeptical. The summer before I left, we were sitting in a bar talking, and I remember the way he spoke about it, emphasizing the "service" component, as in "joining the service," and likening it, incongruously, to his two years in the Army, as if searching for a justification that framed it as something other than the actions of an aimless, spoiled youth avoiding growing up.

Joining the Peace Corps certainly had something to do with that. I prepared my application during the winter of 2000-01, shortly after I had been involved in a car accident that resulted in me having to borrow a large sum of money from my mother. I was depressed, and was stuck in a rut, feeling as if I had no path forward, or, worse, no idea where I wanted to go. Why not go back to Russia? It was something I had wanted to do since my semester in St. Petersburg, in part because of the escapism it offered. Being an American in Russia was easy and intoxicating. I could do that and put off adulthood for a while.

But it wasn't just that. Though there was certainly a degree of avoidance in moving to Russia, I had a feeling that there was something else there apart from cheap beer and the feeling of being a young swashbuckler out in the periphery of the empire. Before I left, as well as while I was there, I kept crossing paths with people whom I had met in St. Petersburg who were building careers in the post-Soviet space, as journalists, as academics, as diplomats, and I thought I could do that too. I began to think that living in Russia was the start of a new life, not the evasion of one.

By the time my parents turned up at the Hotel Moskva, I had concluded that whatever I did in the future - and it was still ill-defined - was going to flow from this period of my life. I had committed myself to doing everything I could to master the language. I read as many Russian novels as I could get my hands on. I started thinking about going back to university when Peace Corps ended. For the first time in my life, I had a direction.

And as I traveled to meet my parents, this was a bit terrifying.

I had a friend in St. Petersburg who quoted a Tolstoy line to me that I always liked: "When a man learns a new language, he becomes another man." I honestly don't know if that's a real Tolstoy quotation, but, regardless, it rang true to me, and I thought about it a lot as my meeting with my parents approached. The life I lived in Russia was a side of me they had never seen, that they didn't know. I had no idea what they'd make of me, not that the old me was gone, but that I was a different person in Russia, I had become another man. I assumed they'd be proud that I was figuring it out. But maybe they'd just be confused.

It was a weird role reversal, interpreting for my parents, watching them like they were bear cubs as we traversed the depths of the Metro in St. Petersburg and Moscow, counselling them on the number of stops until we disembarked, and getting worried they'd be washed away by the waves of humanity cascading into the cars before receding. Or reading the menus for them at restaurants, and giving advice on the various dishes on offer I thought they'd tolerate, the way they used to order one plate of spaghetti and one plate of chicken fingers when we were on long road trips with my sister when I was a child.

Before we went out to Vladimir, I had to buy tickets for the train. There wasn't a straightforward way to do this; you had to have your passport and wait in a bunch of lines at the train station. Rather than have my parents and their friends who came with them stand in line for an extended period of time, I thought they could get a table at the cafe in Kursky Vokzal while I made the arrangements. They couldn't get lost there - at least, I didn't think so. I found them a spot, a green plastic patio table arrayed along the perimeter of the concourse. I told them I'd be back as soon as I could and then walked away, fearful that perhaps I was making a mistake leaving them alone.

*

Interlude: Shitloads of Money

I remember negotiating on behalf of my parents with a *babushka* selling embroidery and lacquer boxes near the Suzdal Kremlin. After I closed the deal, the *babushka* slipped me ten rubles as a commission.

*

When I got back with the tickets, the table was covered with empty beer cans. My parents and their friends had gotten thirsty, and my dad, whose first language was Czech, managed to summon some rudimentary Slavic vocabulary from the depths of his brain to order round after round of beers from a sweet waitress who looked after them while I was standing in line.

It deflated my bubble a bit, but rightfully so. I relaxed after that, no longer desperate to prove or show them anything, just to enjoy their company and try to give them a sense of the place that had come to mean so much to me. We had fun. I insisted on recreating photographs of my mom and me from our first trip to the Soviet Union eleven years before, dragging her to pose in front of St. Basil's Cathedral or Moscow State University. One day in Moscow, my dad and I decided to skip one of the tours in favor of wandering around Aleksandrovsky Garden near the Kremlin. I bought us half liter bottles of beer to drink as we ambled around, before a summer storm blew up and we got soaked by the rain, parading around the gardens, arm in arm, laughing and laughing.

I was wrong about the trip being a collision of worlds. It wasn't.

It was an enrichment of two.

*

When I was a student in St. Petersburg, I went to Estonia as part of the study abroad program I was on. We left late at night from Vitebsky Vokzal. I remember playing *Durak* and drinking beer with my fellow students on the train. Among them was Jenny, who was to become Adam's girlfriend at Georgetown, and who would serve in Peace Corps Russia Far East near Vladivostok while we were in the Western Russia cohort.

The Irony of Fate.

When the train got to the border at the Narva River, I peered out the window. It was dark, but there was enough residual light so that you could see the silhouette of the Ivangorod Fortress, a fifteenth century castle built under orders from Ivan III to counter the threat of the Teutonic Knights, who occupied the imposing Hermann Castle on the opposite bank of the river, in what is now Estonia.

We proceeded through Russian Passport Control, the officials checking our documents and adding the obligatory stamp to our passports. After a time, the train proceeded across the bridge, traveling about a hundred yards before stopping at Estonian Passport Control. The Estonian official took my passport, stamped it, and returned it to me. I opened it to see the Estonian stamp, only to find that the Estonian official had essentially cancelled out the Russian stamp, the ink bleeding into the Russian mark. A few days later, the Russians returned the favor, boxing out the Estonian stamp. When I went to Latvia and back to Estonia while in Peace Corps, the same thing happened. It was like they were playing tic-tac-toe, a passive-aggressive border skirmish taking place on the pages of my passport.

Ленин жив.

*

A few days before I went to Estonia, I was talking to my parents on the phone. My mom got emotional telling me how she remembered the world divided when she was young, and if someone had told her that her son would be going to Estonia, "I have no idea what I would've thought was happening." It was a sweet moment, and I chose not to mention that a few days before, I had been assaulted on the street outside my *obschezhitiye*.

I don't want to know what she would have imagined had she known that one day her son would be beaten up by a Russian.

My parents' generation was very much the Cold War generation, and the Russia they were visiting, the Russia in which I lived, was still very much post-Soviet. Remnants of the Soviet era were commonplace. Perched on top of a building near the college in Vladimir were giant letters spelling out «Слава Труду!» - "Glory to Labor!" I lived on Prospekt Lenina - Lenin Avenue - and the flag of Vladimir Oblast' had - still has - the hammer and sickle on it.

They didn't mention it much, but I know they felt it, and it came out from time to time. In an unguarded moment while we were peering across Red Square, my dad recounted seeing images of Soviet tanks parading across the square on TV when he was a kid, and that he couldn't believe he was standing where he was.

A few months shy of his tenth birthday, in 1950, the local American Legion staged a mock "communist invasion" on May Day in his sleepy little Wisconsin town. The "Communists" arrested the mayor and the parish priest, and detained them behind barbed wire in a hastily erected "concentration camp." The local paper published the day's edition under the banner *The Red Star,* and plastered a portrait of Stalin on the front page. A man who was later to marry one of my dad's cousins was drafted into the "Red Guards," patrolling the streets of the new "United Soviet States of America." One of his first assignments was to corral the nuns from St. Paul's Catholic Church into the "gulag." He carried a pistol. Unlike everything else that day, the pistol was real.

This was the paranoia into which my parents were born and raised. I couldn't help but think of symmetries as they visited Russia, how I came of age at the opposite end of the elongated parabola that was the Cold War, as it was ramping down to what seemed at the time to be a peaceful and optimistic denouement. Or about Ludmilla Anatolovna, born the same year as my mother, recounting to me how she remembered crying when Stalin died, on the other side of the world and divide as my parents.

To a certain extent, you could ignore the weight of history. The trip was mostly about being together again. I was really happy to show them Vladimir - where I lived, where I worked, where I was growing into a new person, a new man, as Tolstoy may or may not have said. But that weight was always there.

One of my favorite photographs from their trip is the three of us sitting arm and arm at the base of the clumsily named 850th Anniversary of Vladimir Monument. It's a three-sided obelisk towering over Cathedral Square. On each side, there is a figure representing the various periods of Vladimir's long history. On one side, there is a *bogatyr* facing down Bolshaya Moskovskaya, towards the Golden Gate, ready to defend the town. The next side is an industrial worker holding a model tractor, in honor of the Vladimir Tractor Factory, named for Zhdanov, recipient of the Order of the Red Banner of Labor. The third side is a medieval architect, admiring the Assumption Cathedral.

Locally, the statue is known as *Tri Duraka* - The Three Fools.

It was constructed in 1958.

A statue of Stalin once stood in the same square.

*

I was really happy in Vladimir. It could be annoying, and stifling at times. But it was a good fit for me.

I loved its many quiet spots - the leafy neighborhood around the Knyaginin Uspensky Monastery, or Pushkin Park near the Assumption Cathedral. I liked to walk to the back corner of the park, high above the Klyazma. You could see a great panorama of the area, starting with the Assumption Cathedral, which I never grew tired of looking at, the Murom Forest stretching off over the horizon, and the terraced streets of the town to the northwest cascading down the hill to the railroad tracks.

I loved Vladimir's understated beauty. I loved watching the sun rise through the arc of the Golden Gate, which cast a brilliant beam of light through the white stone aperture, the way it has for 900 years. I loved seeing the sun reflect off the golden cupolas of the Assumption Cathedral, which created a gilded halo that rose up to heaven. I loved wandering the little alleyways that cut off from Bolshaya Moskovskaya, down which you could find tiny chapels and quiet side streets with views of the Klyazma River and the forest beyond. I loved the way the snow gathered on the melancholy red brick of the Trinity Church.

I loved sitting on the balcony at my place. I didn't know I even had a balcony until the spring, when the frost finally melted off the windows. Once I discovered it, I spent almost every evening out there. I'd take a bottle of beer and my guitar or a book, and breathe in the fresh air. There was a yard adjacent to my building that served as a gathering spot for the residents of the nearby apartment block. It made for good people watching: kids kicking a soccer ball back and forth, *babushki* lugging carpets down from their apartments, hanging them from tree limbs, and bashing them with brooms, plumes of dust emanating with every thrash.

I loved Vladimir's quirky charms. I loved that there were city busses that had been purchased from Germany which still had route maps from Munich posted on the inner walls. I loved watching the flamenco band playing at the Zolotaya Zazhigalka, whose members would drum on their guitars with the palms of their hands when their fingers weren't dancing on the nylon strings and darting up and down the fretboard like a sand crab scampering across the beach. I loved the collection of *babushki* who sold produce outside the *produkty* near my place. They would promise that whatever it was I was making would be better with their preserves or herbs or other homemade delights and I believed them.

I loved the tiny little towns that ringed Vladimir. Everyone once in a while I'd catch a bus that headed east out of the city. It traveled the same route that I took to get to Ludmilla Anatolovna's but instead of turning north on Suzdalsky Prospekt, it kept going east. The bus passed the last of the concrete tower blocks and briefly escaped into the countryside, before coming to a little exurb called Bogolyubovo. Andrei Bogolyubsky built his palace here in the twelfth century, as well as the incomparable Church of the Intercession on the Nerl, one of the most beautiful structures I've ever seen. It stands on the edge of a giant field, tucked down near where the Nerl flows into the Klyazma. At certain times, particularly during the winter, it looks as if it is rising from the earth, stretching its single black cupola and golden Orthodox cross like an outreached hand up towards God, the white stone blending with the snow. Other times it looks as if the earth was fashioned around the church, not the other way around. The knoll on which it stands, the banks of the river, the trees, the sky - they all seemed made to serve the quiet solemnity of its perch, a district of Eden set alongside the river.

I loved going to Suzdal, the little town down the road that time and the Bolsheviks forgot. It was beautiful and peaceful, whether covered in the snow and the long shadows of the winter, or bathed in the sunlight in the spring, when the wildflowers would bloom down along the Kamenka, which geographers ambitiously call a river, but is mostly a small trickle of water lazily gliding past the town. In the spring of 2002, after Ludmilla Anatolovna and I visited a school in town, we were wandering along the Kamenka, near the old kremlin and the Church of the Nativity, its blue, star-spangled cupolas looking like onion-shaped bean bag chairs resting on top of the white stone columns. I remarked how beautiful it was and how much I enjoyed Suzdal. She said, "This whole town is like your dacha. You come here any chance you get." She was right. I feel lucky that when Peace Corps sent me to Vladimir, I got Suzdal for free.

For all of my initial misgivings about the place, I felt like I belonged in Vladimir, like it had become a part of me. When we were leaving Russia in 2003, Marina, who worked in the Moscow office, handed me a farewell note. It read, "I will always remember you as a Russia-American Владимировец."

A Russia-American Владимировец.

That's what I had become.

**

Exile

Being in the Peace Corps in Western Russia was a pretty cushy assignment. For the most part, it was possible to create a semblance of my life back home. I drank beer in bars. I was able to buy records by the Strokes and Beck and Etta James. There were no large insects, or tropical diseases, or insurgents threatening to march on the capital to worry about. It got cold, sure, and the war in Chechnya occasionally spilled out of the Caucasus, but in the age of September 11th, something like the *Nord-Ost* theater siege wasn't terribly different than what was going on back home. During the presentation in Training about the emergency evacuation protocols, my friends and I sat in the back joking about whether we were ever going to practice grabbing onto the struts of a helicopter taking off from the roof of the Embassy, and which documents to burn before we swallowed our Peace Corps-issued cyanide ampoules should the KGB show up on our doorstep. We had the privilege to be snarky.

Though it was unlikely we were going to have to flee while under fire from distant artillery, that's not to say we were secure. We didn't know it at the time, but we were the last group to ever serve in Russia. The end of Peace Corps in Russia wasn't dramatic. It was slow, fragmented, individual volunteers leaving from Perm', from Velikiye Luki, from Kolomna, one by one. It played out over a year and began before we even got there. As we were arriving in Moscow, another planeload of Volunteers departed, heading in the other direction. They were members of

Group VIII. They hadn't received visa extensions to stay in the country. Nobody at the Moscow office was sure why. But we were oblivious to this. If there was any concern, it wasn't apparent to us.

That changed once we got to site. In addition to the steady trickle of Volunteers going home, the Moscow office started to hint that our position in Russia was more precarious than we had been led to believe. Newspaper reports cited unnamed or low-level Russian officials suggesting we were unqualified, or up to something nefarious, posing as "Volunteers" when in actuality we were "former officers of the American security services." It was laughable, but indicated there was a possibility that we would all suffer the same fate as the group before us, that some - or all - of us would be sent home before our time was up. The summer seemed to be the most likely collision point. Our visas were set to expire. It was an open question whether we would get renewed or not.

Throughout that winter and spring, there were lots of stories of Volunteers being harassed by local officials. In April 2002, I sent a frantic email to my parents telling them to hold off planning their trip to see me. The local ОВИР had notified me that my registration in town was being reconsidered, and I had to scramble to be allowed to stay. It got worked out, but it was a shot across the bow. I told my parents that their visit to me had to be before my visa expired that August.

On August 8th, Melanie and I caught the train into Moscow. Everybody was converging at the Peace Corps office. We'd find out whether we made it or not. Those who did would head to Riga to get their visas renewed. Those who didn't would go home. I remember I had a fair amount of resignation about the whole thing. I had jokingly said to my parents at the end of their visit a few days before, "See you soon," but the accompanying laughter was nervous. I didn't want to leave. It would've been a tremendous letdown.

When we got to the office, the lists were posted in the Volunteer Common Room. It was surreal, standing next to the makeshift library, a gigantic bowl of condoms, and a portrait of a smirking George W. Bush on the wall, as I scanned the list tacked on a door to discover my fate. I didn't stall, or look for others first. I just wanted to know. I found my name. I turned to Melanie.

"I made it."

"I made it too."

We embraced. I took a deep breath and started scanning the list again to find the fate of my friends. Chris - yes. Simon - yes. Rob - yes. Andrew - yes.

Laura - no.

Adam - no.

"Oh."

"No."

*

Our group had been slashed in half. There was no pattern to who did and who did not survive. It wasn't all Volunteers in one city, or one region, or anything like that. It was random, with just a touch of gratuitous assholery thrown in to remind us who was in charge: married couples were split, one partner made it, one didn't.

Other Volunteers filtered in and out of the office, to check the list, shake hands with and hug those who were staying or leaving. I was genuinely happy for those who were staying and genuinely sad for those going home. I felt, and feel, a deep connection to everyone in our group, which made it all the more bittersweet. The band was breaking up.

No sooner had I started to mentally process that I was going to be able to stay another year, Elena came into the room.

"*Dooglas*, Melanie. There's a problem."

*

Several of us left to go grab a drink. Out on Schmitovsky Passazh, we ran into Adam and Laura. "I didn't make it," said Laura, with a bit of a smile on her face. She didn't seem too broken up about it, but Adam was bummed. So was I. Adam and Laura leaving was different than when other comrades had gone. I was sad when Texas Mike went home, but losing Laura and Adam was like having a tooth pulled. There was going to be negative space to remind you of the whole that no longer was.

We had a few days before we were to go to Riga, and we spent that time lobbying Laura and Adam to come with us anyway. Laura declined but we convinced Adam. There was time for one more adventure. Once in Latvia, we went to the beach at Jūrmala and then spent a marvelous day in a park in Riga, lying in the grass, drinking Aldaris beer, and doing nothing but playing endless hands of *Durak* and laughing. After months of feeling like I was in perpetual mental and physical motion, it was nice to just sit still and watch the world go by.

It was a reprieve, but only just that. The next day, Adam went back to Russia one last time and the rest of us - Melanie, Chris, Simon, Rob, Andrew, and I - continued on to Vilnius. Before Adam left, he reached into his bag and handed me a bottle of vodka that he had bought when he was visiting Jenny in Vladivostok earlier that year.

"For a special occasion."

"We'll drink it together."

"Maybe."

And then he got on the train.

*

Interlude: It Tolls for Thee

I remember playing a continuous game of *Durak* while traveling in Latvia and Lithuania. Chris, Simon, Andrew, Rob and I developed a scheme to cheat in order to make Melanie the *durak* over and over and over again. The more frustrated she got, the less she paid attention, and so our cheating got more and more brazen and overt, to the point that we were openly showing each other our hands in order to coordinate our moves. When Melanie finally realized this, she stopped talking to us for about an hour or so.

She eventually forgave us.

I think.

*

"Dooglas, Melanie. There's a problem."

After we returned from the Baltics, Melanie and I went back to Vladimir for the last time.

The problem that Elena had referred to was this: authorities in Vladimir, acting on their own accord, had expelled us from the town. If Moscow wasn't going to kick us out, they'd do it themselves. The stated reasons - that there was no more room at the *obschezhitiye* for Melanie and that my college could no longer pay the rent for my room - were obviously bullshit. This was driven home when the initial idea to relocate me to Murom was scratched because it was located in Vladimirskaya Oblast', and Peace Corps had reason to believe I'd be denied permission to live there too. Some faceless bureaucrat at the city or oblast' level - the ОВИР, the FSB - wanted us gone, and so we were.

Peace Corps immediately decided to send Melanie to Uglich. For some reason, I was given a choice. I could go to Kaluga, a small, Vladimir-sized town southwest of Moscow, or Ekaterinburg, a massive city in the Urals I had always wanted to visit. It wasn't a difficult decision. But it was a lot to take in.

I mostly ignored it while traveling in Latvia and Lithuania. While we were in Riga, I remember quizzing Larissa, who worked in the Moscow office, on the proper pronunciation of "Ekaterinburg," but apart from that, I put it out of my mind. I wasn't in denial. We were having too much fun, and in any event, I didn't know what to think. It was only when we got back to Moscow that I couldn't ignore it anymore. Simon, Rob, Andrew - they all went back to site to resume their lives. Melanie and I went back to Vladimir to cram ours into as few suitcases and bags as we could.

A few days later, Kolya picked me up in a Peace Corps Land Cruiser. I loaded my stuff in and we set off. We drove up Prospekt Lenina, and turned onto Builders Street. We had one more stop. We headed north from the city center towards the university where Melanie lived. This time, she was coming with us. We packed her things next to mine and Kolya pulled away from the curb. Ten months before, we had been met on the platform at the *vokzal* by our future colleagues and students, snow swirling in the air above our rising breath. This time, it was a hot summer day, and the Land Cruiser kicked up dust as we turned onto the highway towards Moscow. There were no pictures, no send off, no ceremony. I didn't even turn around and watch the outskirts of the city recede from view.

We just left.

As far as the Vladimir authorities were concerned, the problem was solved.

*

Melanie and I had our own Vladimir experiences, but much of my life during those ten months was intertwined with her, so much so that when we were pulled apart, I was like a disbalanced top, spinning away uncontrollably.

My memories of Melanie in Vladimir aren't marked by individual episodes. Being with her was more like breathing, each breath insignificant on its own, but, simultaneously, each one as essential as the next, as the last, essential in its own right. We never went very long without seeing each other, much like I couldn't go very long without oxygen. No matter how I was feeling - and I experienced just about every human emotion there is while in Vladimir - dropping by Melanie's was a way to come up for air.

I could catalogue dozens of vignettes from our time together in Vladimir, but that seems reductive and unnecessary, as if our friendship relied on a preponderance of evidence to be real, as if describing the contours of the universe required counting all of its stars. My friendship with Melanie was about presence as much as anything, and whatever personal growth I was able to achieve in Russia happened in a large part because I knew I had her to back me up, to give me a kick in the ass when I needed it, to offer support, or just companionship in a place that lent itself to loneliness even when there were lots of people around. Solace was just a five-ruble *marshrutka* ride away.

*

Interlude: The Encyclopedia of Plague and Pestilence

I remember when Melanie contracted giardiasis after she and I visited St. Petersburg because I had assured her it was fine to use the tap water to brush her teeth. She stayed for a few days at a hospital in Vladimir whose conditions seemed to match those of a triage station on the Eastern Front.

She eventually forgave me.

I think.

*

During Peace Corps gatherings, there was usually some sort of show. The staff would recruit Volunteers to sing or play an instrument or do some other performance. Andrew wowed us with his piano playing at the end of Training, and Noteboom was always good to grab a guitar and belt out "Runaround Sue" or "Friends in Low Places." Even Melanie got in on the act, singing folk songs with a couple of other Volunteers. It was cool, but it wasn't my thing. I didn't even reveal to my friends that I played guitar for a while because I didn't want to get roped into performing.

As our Mid-Service Training conference in March approached, Melanie and I had some discussions about biting the bullet and volunteering ourselves as an act. We figured we might get drafted into it and thought it would be good to be prepared. We tossed around a couple of song ideas, but the one we kept coming back to was "Landslide." I messed around with it on guitar but we never got to the point of actually rehearsing together. When we got to the conference, I picked up the guitar and sang "Folsom Prison Blues."

It was a time of growth I guess.

Though we didn't sing it together, "Landslide" was a good choice, not only because it's a great song, but that it cuts to the essence of what Melanie was for me, even if I didn't appreciate it until later. It is, of course, a song about a breakup. Melanie and I weren't an item, but we were destined to be driven apart nonetheless. When it happened, few words were as apt as:

I've been afraid of changing
Because I've built my life around you

When the threads of our life together in Vladimir were pulled apart, to the extent that I was able to right myself - eventually - it was because I knew that Melanie was going through the same thing. I could see my reflection in the snow-covered hills, and I didn't want the landslide to bring me down. True, I couldn't hop into a careening *marshrutka* and speed off to her *obschezhitiye* to fill my lungs with oxygen anymore, "but time makes you bolder, even children get older."

I had learned, from her, how to breathe on my own.

I'm getting older too.

*

Melanie left for Uglich immediately. I hung out in Moscow with Chris, who was in town after spending a few days back in Zelenograd visiting his host family. We went to a giant *rynok* that sold pirated CDs. I bought Bruce Springsteen's *The Ghost of Tom Joad, The Piper at the Gates of Dawn* by Pink Floyd, a record by a Russian band called Сплин, and a compilation of Glenn Gould playing piano sonatas by Beethoven.

The next day, Chris left to head back to Verkhoturye. A silver lining to all of this upheaval was that he and I were going to be relatively close to one another. His site was about 150 miles from Ekaterinburg. We made plans for him to come visit me in a couple of weeks, after I got settled in.

I didn't go out or do anything that last night in Moscow. I stayed, alone, at the Peace Corps guest apartment, trying to visualize my new life, but of course I didn't know where to start. If my visions from the year before were romantic and idealistic, now they were just muddled and ill-defined. I couldn't envision myself in Ekaterinburg. What was the city like? Who was I going to hang out with? How was I going to get around? What was

I going to teach? I didn't know the answers to those questions the year before - or even which questions to ask - but I didn't care then. That was the exciting part. Now all I could do was to try to bring focus to that lack of definition, a fool's errand if there ever was one, like trying to pull water out of a glass with your hand.

But if my emotions about everything were nebulous, there was room for excitement among all the uncertainty. Ekaterinburg was a city I had always wanted to visit. It seemed to be a pretty cool place.

Maybe this will be a good thing.

Maybe.

*

The next day, Misha, one of the Peace Corps drivers, picked me up in a Peace Corps Land Cruiser. I loaded my stuff in and we set off. We drove up the Garden Ring towards Kazansky Vokzal. The Garden Ring was smothered in traffic as always. As we slowly rounded a bend, wedged into our lane by Volgas and Zhigulis and the odd Mercedes, the song "The Final Countdown" came on the radio. Misha, without saying a word, rolled down the windows and cranked it up, synthesizers blasting out a soundtrack for Moscow rush hour traffic.

When we got to the *vokzal*, Misha helped me carry my stuff to the platform. He loaded all of it onto the train. I had two second class berths, one for me, one for my things.

I looked at the tickets: Moscow - Sverdlovsk. I smiled. Sverdlovsk was the Soviet name for Ekaterinburg.

Ленин жив.

"Good luck, *Dooglas!*"

Misha offered me his hand and I shook it.

Then I climbed aboard.

When Yuri Gagarin was shot into space in 1961, sitting in a capsule on top of a Vostok-K rocket, he announced his liftoff with a remarkable understatement - *Поехали!* - Let's go! - as if going into orbit was like going to the beach. Or Sverdlovsk.

My final countdown wasn't of quite the same magnitude, but it was close enough. I sat down in my berth, looked out the window, and waited for the train to roll.

Moscow – Sverdlovsk

Поехали.

*

The train jostled to a start and pulled out of the station. We rolled through Moscow, rocking back and forth on the wide Russian-gauge track. I mostly gazed out the window, lost in thought. The train ride to Ekaterinburg was to last twenty-six hours. I had time to settle in and think about what was to come.

For all the butterflies in my stomach at that moment, my most immediate concern was that our path was likely to take us through Vladimir. Many routes to the east from Moscow went via Vladimir; that had been the case since Tsarist times, when exiles were force-marched down the Vladimirka to god knows where. I steeled myself for our arrival, to see the Assumption Cathedral one last time, dominating the bluffs above the tracks, which ran along the Klyazma. It was like coming face-to-face with an old girlfriend who had broken my heart. I thought maybe I'd look away, not meet Vladimir's gaze, pretend I didn't even notice I was passing through, just one town in a hundred on my way to the Urals, another nowhere in Podmoskovye, not even worth photographing in 1991.

Or maybe I'd face up to it. I didn't look at the timetable, but if we were going to stop in Vladimir, maybe I'd disembark, and walk up and down the platform, the platform where ten months before I had begun the life that had been so cruelly snatched from me, and look at my fellow - or former - or fellow - compatriots, Владимировци all of them - all of us - all of them, and I'd see Ludmilla Anatolovna, and Anya, and Polina - *Как здорово! Что все мы здесь! Сегодня собрались!* - and Maksim with his two beers - *Давай зажигаем!* - and his dad in the swamped *Ooooaaazzz Rrrrrrrussian Dzheep* spilling cigarette butts and the waters of the Klyazma onto the concrete, and the faceless bureaucrat who kicked me and Melanie out - *Как здорово!* - and the armies of Batu Khan, and the Three Fools, and the workers of the Vladimir Tractor Factory named for Zhdanov with their Order of the Red Banner of Labor, and the ladies who recognized me at the pirozhki place on Bolshaya Moskovskaya, and *fooking* Semyon and Dasha and Nastya and Zhenya and Marina, and Lenin, though he lives - *Ленин жив!* - in Ekaterinburg too, and all of my neighbors, two of whom didn't give a shit whether I was leaving or staying, one wishing me luck using the formal construction and giggling as the cork from a bottle of Sovetskoe champagne launches into the air, and one reciting the poetry of Pushkin in a Skirt. She wrote:

> I used to think that after we are gone
> there's nothing, simply nothing at all.
> Then who's that wandering by the porch

again and calling us by name?
Whose face is pressed against the frosted pane?
What hand out there is waving like a branch?

Also:

Tonight I pine for no one,
alone in my candlelit room;
but I don't-don't-don't want to know
who's kissing whom.

Все мы здесь!
As it was, our train went down another track.
Сегодня собрались!
We went through Murom instead.
"*Dooglas,* give me your camera."
The Irony of Fate.

*

Interlude: The Stationmaster

I remember Dima pointing to me as my train arrived in
Ekaterinburg. Dima pointed with confidence, knowing it
was me that he was to meet (perhaps my fearful eyes gave
me away). I remember going to my apartment with him
and another dude who I never saw again.

I remember how utterly alone I felt when ~~the students from the college and Anya and Polina~~ *Dima and another dude who I never saw again* left that first night in ~~Vladimir~~ *Ekaterinburg*. I ~~remember warming up the pork chops that Tamara sent with me~~ *don't remember what I ate. Probably just snacks from the train.* I remember reading ~~Novel with Cocaine~~ *Woody Guthrie: A Life* those first few weeks. ~~I remember making arrangements while on the train in transit to meet with Melanie at the Golden Gate a few days after we arrived.~~ *Melanie was in Uglich. Uglich was 830 miles away. Melanie was 830 miles away.*

It was considerably less fun the second time, being whisked across an unfamiliar city from the train station, being deposited in an empty room, being left, alone, with vague instructions about where to go and when to meet some people, to get situated. I was tired from the train ride and worn down from the stress of the past several days. I made the bed and collapsed into it.

When I woke up the next morning, I set out to explore. I lived in an *obschezhitiye* attached to the university where I was going to work, the impressively named Ural State University of Railway Transportation. My place was nice, certainly more comfortable than where I lived in Vladimir. I had my own kitchen and bathroom, and the main room was spacious enough. I made myself a cup of coffee and got to work getting my bearings. Gazing out the window, I could see the main line of the railroad cutting through a sea of residential concrete. Beyond the railroad was the industrial northern suburbs of the city.

There wasn't much of note in the immediate vicinity. There were a few other *obschezhitiyes* like mine nearby, and the university complex was just down the street, a huge Brutalist monolith dominating the shore of the Iset River. The neighborhood was hemmed in by the river to the south and the main rail line to the north. Though fairly close to the city center, it always felt a bit isolated. It was in a transportation blind spot. I had to walk a quarter mile to catch a bus, and even then, due to the geography and street plan, it was usually quicker to walk a mile to the nearest subway stop to get downtown.

I was pretty anxious to have a look around. The weather had already started to turn when I arrived and rather than take this as a portentous sign about the coming winter, I was relieved, as the last month in Vladimir had been unpleasantly hot. I threw on my jacket, grabbed my bag, and walked out the door.

*

Interlude: По Улице Иду Я, По Улице - Один

I went for a very long walk on a weekend in Ekaterinburg for the sole purpose of walking to Ulitsa Chapaeva. I ran into the very pretty tennis-playing student I tutored while doing so.

*

Ekaterinburg is really different from Vladimir. It's a vibrant metropolis. It has an active music scene, lots of museums, and plenty of nightlife. I didn't know how to tap into those things, and didn't know anyone who could show me around, but I figured that would work itself out, and I had initial excitement to explore the place. I spent the first few days and weeks in town expanding the radius around my neighborhood, exploring the city. I'd look at a map while drinking coffee in the morning and choose a destination; a street that sounded interesting, or the zoo, or the US Consulate, or the drama theater. It didn't really matter. It was just a waypoint to guide my wanderings.

Ekaterinburg is probably the most Soviet city I've lived in. It had a touch of the imperial grandeur of St. Petersburg, but so much of it is Socialist Neoclassicism. Its avenues are punctuated by statues of Bolsheviks - Lenin, Sverdlov, Malyshev - all coming together at 1905 Square, which is dominated by the city Duma, a Stalinist hunk of concrete which looks like the headpiece of one of the Seven Sisters that tower over Moscow.

Tucked among all the grandeur were some cool spots. There's a linear park that ran the length of much of Prospekt Lenina that reminded me of Tverskoi Bulvar in Moscow. Someone painted a life-sized reproduction of Matisse's *La Danse* on a wall in an underpass downtown. A few blocks away there was an electronics store that sold jazz records. Encased in the glass display was a copy of *Mingus Ah Um* that I eventually bought myself for Christmas. Its 1,500 ruble price tag seemed prohibitive when I first saw it, but I knew one day I'd cave. I used to go visit it, like it was a pet I had adopted that I wasn't allowed to bring home yet. Nearby was a monument to the citizens of Ekaterinburg who died in the war in Afghanistan that was remarkably solemn. It depicts a soldier, sitting on the ground, hunched over, clutching a Kalashnikov, looking absolutely defeated. It's a striking contrast to the creepy triumphalism of all the Brezhnev-era World War II memorials that make up the focal point of Russian cities large and small. A short jaunt away was where the Bolsheviks murdered Nicholas II and his family in 1918. When I was there they were in the process of constructing the Church on Blood in Honor of All Saints Resplendent in the Russian Land, the garbled mouthful of a name for the commemorative cathedral that was built on the site. I remember watching a crane hoisting the gold cupolas into place one of the last weekends I was in town.

I'd also ride to random Metro stops to walk around. I went to every one in the city, which isn't all that impressive, because there were only seven when I lived there, the last of which, Geologicheskaya, opened on New Year's Day 2003. I went to check it out on a very hungover sojourn on opening day. The whole city had the same idea. The Metro stations weren't as grand as those in Moscow or St. Petersburg but they were cool nonetheless. Most of them were sleek, with steel, and mirrors, and modern chandeliers, their interior walls lined with multicolored geologic specimens collected from the Urals. The interior of Uralmash Station, named for the Stalinist industrial complex that was built in the 1930s as part of the scorched-earth industrialization of the Five Year Plans, had metal helixes winding overhead that looked like the threads of a giant screw. My favorite station was Prospekt Kosmonavtov, which combined Futuristic mosaics and bas-reliefs with Art Deco light fixtures and mirrored columns to create a reflective space extravaganza.

As the weather got colder, I'd plan my wandering with a little more care so I'd have a place I knew to drop into to warm up with a cup of coffee, or maybe a beer. There was a Subway near the Central Post Office that had Baltika on draft and played reggae videos on the TVs hanging from the ceiling. MakPik, the local McDonald's knockoff, had a location near 1905 Square that I frequented. I'd drink coffee and watch the trams go up and down Prospekt Lenina. Occasionally, I'd hop a random tram and ride for a while as it snaked out of the city center to the residential areas beyond. After a while, I'd get out and ride the inbound back downtown. When I got tired, I'd take the Metro back to Dinamo, the station closest to where I lived, or just walk along City Pond until I got back to the university.

So many of my memories of Ekaterinburg are sad, but that's the fault of circumstance. It's a really cool town and I'm glad I got to see so much of it.

*

Soon after I arrived, I dropped by the university to meet my counterparts and find out what my responsibilities were to be. They were a husband and wife team - Boris and Elena Ivanovna. Boris was an instructor and rector at the university, and Elena Ivanovna ran the English-language program in which I was to teach. I liked them both. During those first few weeks, I spent a lot of time sitting in Boris' office, drinking tea with him. He had very strong opinions about certain varieties of green tea, on which he was happy to expound at length. He would brew up several different cups for me at a time, and as I tried each, he would explain to me all of the subtleties and flavor notes, which I pretended to notice and appreciate.

Elena Ivanovna was kind and sweet. She was a bit like Tamara and Ludmilla Anatolovna, but with a softer touch, less intense, though she had no qualms about telling me when I was doing it wrong if she thought it necessary. Like Tamara and Ludmilla Anatolovna, and most Russian women of her generation, Elena Ivanovna was a vicarious hypochondriac and an amateur virologist, and linked any ailment I ever had to a specific irresponsible practice that I was going to have to discontinue for my own survival. When I caught a cold in October, she reasoned it was because I had been wearing my denim jacket instead of something warmer, and she insisted I call the Peace Corps doctor in Moscow for advice. When I protested that that was ridiculous, that it was *just a cold*, she handed me the phone and stared at me wordlessly until I gave in and dialed. Several months later, she warned me against going outside when the temperature was forecast to drop towards minus forty. Any protestation I'd offer would be met with, "I need you healthy."

Dooglas.
Please.

*

When I first met with Elena Ivanovna soon after my arrival, she said two things to me. The first was, "Your work will be easy, but there will be a lot of it." And then she said that she was still on summer break and I should come back next week.

My first month in Ekaterinburg was marked by its idleness. There wasn't anything for me to do. If there was a promise of "a lot" of work eventually, in the beginning there was none. My classes weren't scheduled to begin until October. I filled the time during the week by tutoring a couple of students and doing aimless research about a grant Elena Ivanovna wanted me to write, but that was it. I'd get up, walk over to the university, and sit at a computer, staring at the screen, occasionally punctuating this inaction by drinking cups of tea with Boris.

There were two reasons for this. The first is that the university wasn't expecting to have a Volunteer that year, and therefore didn't have anything lined up for me to do before the term began. They had been hosting Volunteers for a while, so it's not that they were new to the relationship. I assume that when things fell apart in Vladimir and Peace Corps needed to find a new posting for me, they called up Boris and Elena Ivanovna and asked for a favor, and they obliged. But summer break is summer break.

The second reason is that my motivation and morale was low, and it plummeted further as the month dragged on. Despite some initial excitement I had about starting over in Ekaterinburg, my disposition quickly devolved into one of self-pity. I'd think back to the same period in Vladimir, flush with excitement at being at site, ready to jump into my new life. It was such a contrast to what I was feeling in Ekaterinburg, and I quickly fell into that fatal spiral of feeling sorry for myself, writing, pathetically, in an email home, "Why do I have to go through this shit again?"

*

Attempts to extricate myself from this stupor were unsuccessful, although at times I wasn't trying very hard. Apart from Elena Ivanovna and Boris, I knew exactly one person in the city, a student from the university named Dima, who had picked me up at the *vokzal* when I got into town. I'll never forget seeing Dima as my train pulled alongside the platform. I was looking out of the window, unsure of who or what I was looking for. When I arrived in Vladimir, I knew Polina and Anya were waiting for me. My welcoming party in Ekaterinburg was theoretical and ill-defined. I knew someone would be there, but who they were or what they looked like was a mystery. It didn't take long to figure it out. As the train decelerated, and my eyes darted from person to person to person, blank faces arrayed across the platform, they settled on Dima, whose intense stare met my gaze. It was like our eyes locked onto each other. He was pointing directly at me, his arm cocked so that the pistol that was his hand rested at eye-level, as if he were aiming at me down the sight. The barrel followed me laterally until the train came to a halt and I was a moving target no more.

Dima and a few others took me back to my place, and after I was deposited in the *obschezhitiye*, he told me he'd be back to show me around. He took me to the university and introduced me to Boris and a few other people. We hung out a few times over the next few months, but for whatever reason, we just never clicked. I'll admit I didn't make as much effort as I could have to develop a friendship of sorts, writing to my friend Nate, "I am just in this antisocial funk, not wanting to make any effort to meet people."

And so I didn't.

But I had another idea. By this point Laura Jean was back in America. Somebody needed to play sad songs.

And so I did.

*

Kick the shit out of town
They dragged you to the ground
Now you've got nothing, nothing to lose

Break the glass cut your hand
Smear the blood across your skin
Now you've got nothing, nothing to lose

Send me a postcard from Rhode Island again
Send me a postcard from Rhode Island again

Light a match touch the fuse
Turn your house to barbecue
Now you've got nothing, nothing to lose

Meet your girl break her heart
Drive your car down the boulevard
Now you've got nothing, nothing to lose

Send me a postcard from Rhode Island again
Send me a postcard from Rhode Island again

-        Ekaterinburg, 2002

Midway through my service, during the summer of 2002, I was denied the right to live in the city of Vladimir. I was kicked out of town. The politics of this weren't personal or tied to anything I did or didn't do. Some faceless local bureaucrat decided that Melanie and I were no longer welcome. We were the shit. We had to go.

Though the decision may not have been personal, I certainly took it that way. I was devastated and despondent, heartbroken and scared when it happened. When I arrived back in town from Moscow with only a few days to gather my things and settle my affairs, I was so confused and hurt and rudderless. All of this was made worse by the fact that I had very few people with whom to grieve. My friends, Anya and Polina, were both away. I had dinner with Ludmilla Anatolovna and Slava, but it was like a wake. I had the unenviable task of gathering all of the items people had so generously lent me - a carpet, a bunch of pots and pans, some books - and lugging them across town to the college, their owners all away on holiday, oblivious to the fact that I was leaving town forever. I wasn't afforded the opportunity to say goodbye, or thank them for being so nice to me.

The only person still around was the head of the English department, Ludmilla Leonidovna. She really disliked me. I don't blame her for that. She was old, and raised in a system that portrayed Americans as the enemy. And one time I corrected her English in front of a student and I don't think she ever forgave me for that. She muttered under her breath «Мне не нужен американец» - I don't need an American - perhaps forgetting, perhaps not, that I could understand what she was saying. Needless to say, if I was looking for someone who would miss me, I wasn't going to find it with her. I dropped the items off in her office and left.

I had kept my shit together up until that point, but afterwards I broke down. I walked through the park behind the college and pathetically bought a pack of cigarettes I had no intention of smoking. I sat down on the ground and wept. Just a few months before I had walked through the same park with Zhenya and Nastya and Marina and Dasha and *fooking* Semyon, my former students who were becoming my friends. I remember cracking a joke in Russian about mosquitoes that landed. They all laughed. It felt like an arrival. Sitting in the empty park, alone, about to leave it for the last time - I was speechless and spent.

That was the genesis of this song, though I didn't try to capture it until several months later. The line about nothing left to lose isn't in the metaphorical sense. It was that I literally had nothing. My friends, my job, my home, my Russian identity. It was all gone. I had lost everything.

The refrain is a reference to my friend Nate writing to me about a trip he took to Rhode Island. He didn't actually send a postcard. But I remember thinking how unreal the semblance of a normal summer life back in America felt to me at the time. He was going to Rhode Island. I was dispatched on a train headed east to a town I'd never been to, to be met by people I didn't know.

And it wasn't my choice.

Interlude: A Hero of Our Time

Dima would point out a professor "Пышкин," who was not "Пушкин."

*

Soon after I arrived, I checked in at the US Consulate. Ekaterinburg was a big enough city to warrant an international presence, and there was a mini-embassy row, lined with the missions from the USA and the Czech Republic. Peace Corps had let them know I was coming to town and I wandered over to introduce myself and give them my contact information should they need it for whatever reason. The Consulate was tucked away on Ulitsa Gogolya, a few blocks off of Malysheva. When I dropped by, the place was barricaded behind concrete blocks stretched across the road. It was around the first anniversary of September 11th and security was pretty tight. I didn't have much contact with them again until November, when they invited me to Thanksgiving dinner. I caught a taxi and we drove through a blizzard across the city, the Lada slipping and sliding and skidding in the snow.

The taxi dropped me off, I made my way inside, and was introduced around. Most of the staff were pretty junior FSOs on their first or second tour, not much older than me. I got the sense that Ekaterinburg was a pretty unsexy assignment, and their disappointment was palpable. They had visions of a career in exotic or glamorous locales, and stamping visas in an industrial city in the Urals wasn't what they had in mind. I couldn't help but contrast myself with them, how we had similar backgrounds and desires to see the world but took entirely different paths.

Their lives seemed so alien to mine. A big topic of conversation was that their stash of Pilsner Urquell beer was running low, and one of them was going to have to negotiate with the Czechs at the consulate next door to arrange another shipment, and *it's got to be someone else because I did it last time*. Another kept going on about his Seasonal Affective Disorder that was triggered by the winter. I sympathized, but the way he spoke about it had a tone that implied that he didn't *deserve* to have it, and if he had gotten the posting he had wanted, if only he wasn't stuck in this godforsaken dark and cold hellscape in *fucking Russia* . . .

One of them asked me about where I lived and I mentioned that I hadn't had hot water for a few weeks. There was an awkward silence, which someone broke by inviting me to hang out the following weekend. I think they felt sorry for me.

I wasn't exactly pleading poverty, though they may have taken it as such. I had some discomforts to contend with, but nothing serious. Washing my clothes by hand in a basin was burdensome, but after a while I stopped thinking about it that way. I was listening to a lot of Bruce Springsteen at the time, and one lyric resonated with me:

"You get used to anything - sooner or later it just becomes your life."

Washing clothes by hand, boiling water in order to have a shower when the hot water was turned off periodically and unexpectedly, being crammed into the interior of a bus so tight that I couldn't move - sooner or later that just became my life.

My situation wasn't particularly dire - if I wanted to pack it in, all I had to do was pick up the phone and I'd be on an airplane home - but I did milk my relative hardship with the Consulate folks. I felt, as a Peace Corps Volunteer, I had an image to live up to, and took a bit of pleasure in making the junior diplomats feel soft.

*

Note: "Picking up the phone," while simple in the grand scheme of things, was actually a bit complicated. I never had a phone in either of the places where I lived. If I wanted to talk to anyone on the phone, I had to walk across town to the telephone exchange, and pay in advance to sit in a booth and talk for a couple of minutes until I ran out of time, at which point the line would disconnect, sometimes in mid-sentence.

Sooner or later it just becomes your life.

*

Interlude: Guess I'm Doing Fine

Beck's *Sea Change* was for sale at a kiosk near city hall in Ekaterinburg for two months before I finally bought it two months too late.

Snow, snow, cover the marigolds
Breathe, breathe, breathe
So my cheeks they don't freeze
So my skin it don't break and I bleed
From my head to my heart to my knees

Kiss, kiss, kiss from your calf to your knee
Knee, kiss from your knee to your thigh, breathe
I won't let the ice freeze
Your knee through your heart to your eye

I, I'll switch off the lights
And you'll close, close the door
Before we've shed all our
Clothes strewn around
All we left in this town
Were our names
Carved outside in the snow

-        Ekaterinburg, 2002

In March 2002, Liz and I took a trip to Nizhny Novgorod. I remember we somehow missed our train from Vladimir and wound up traveling by bus. As we were walking from the bus station to our hotel, we passed a broad square with a formidable Lenin statue, which attracted our mocking attention. We were walking past the statue making jokes, when a powerful gust of wind blew across the square and knocked the both of us over, and almost pushed us into the street. I remember seeing the blurred wheels of a passing beige Lada spinning a few feet from my head.

Ленин жив.

I remember really seeing the Volga River for the first time soon after. This was very meaningful to me. I'd crossed over it on trains between St. Petersburg and Moscow, but standing on its banks was different. It's like the Mississippi River. It's not just a river. It's an idea, a character, a setting, a myth, an artery that connects more than geography, but history and identity as well. Afterwards, every time I crossed the Volga I made sure to be aware, even if that meant waking or staying up late at night on a train.

The hotel we stayed at was called the Волжкий Откос. Liz found the hotel and made the arrangements and reservation on a recommendation from someone at the American Home. It felt like we were the only people staying in the place and the long corridors gave off a vibe reminiscent of some Soviet take on *The Shining.*

Nizhny Novgorod was a cool town. I remember walking to Gorky's childhood home, and trying to find the Sakharov Museum (which was closed), and standing on a bluff high above the Oka River. It was probably thirty below and felt every bit of it.

The song is a document from that trip, though I wrote it months later, after Liz and I had broken up. The marigolds line came first, mostly because I saw snow covering some flowers near where I lived in Ekaterinburg, though I couldn't tell you if they were marigolds or not. It seemed like a nice turn of phrase. I remember I messed around with the rhythm of the lines a lot, adding the "breathe" parts to mark time and establish meter and then leaving them in there because they were evocative. At one point they served as literal reminders to breathe, as the lines and the melody stretched longer and longer, though they eventually turned out manageable.

This is one of the best songs I wrote while I was in Russia.

*

Interlude: The World is Sverdlovskaya Oblast'

I remember after Chris had come to visit me in Ekaterinburg a few times thinking that I would like to visit Verkhoturye. A few days before a long weekend that Chris and I had agreed to get together for, I called him to make arrangements, thinking I would suggest me going there, rather than vice versa. A woman answered at the hotel where he lived and I asked for Chris. I could hear his heavy footsteps as he walked to the phone. "Get me out of this fucking hellhole," he said. I never did go to Verkhoturye.

*

Chris was off the grid.

He was probably the most isolated of all of us. His town, Verkhoturye, is a tiny monastery town tucked away in the Ural Mountains. There wasn't anyone near him. Melanie and I had each other. Laura was in Penza with a bunch of other Volunteers. Adam was in Volgograd, and although the other Volunteer in the city was an old man we called Wild Bill, Adam seemed fine. Even Simon, who was sent to a tiny village out in Siberia, was relatively close to Krasnoyarsk, where Rob and Andrew and a few others lived. We all had support systems. Chris didn't even have internet. When we went out to site in October, he vanished into the hinterland. We made jokes about Chris showing up at our Mid-Service Training conference in March with a long beard, like Rasputin, who, incidentally, spent some time in Verkhoturye, where he underwent a spiritual awakening and swore off meat and alcohol.

Chris certainly didn't undertake any sort of monastic conversion to ascetic self-denial while in Verkhoturye. Unlike Rasputin, he spent the winter drinking and listening to punk rock, which he probably would have done no matter where he was. That's not to say he was happy. He'd never admit it, nor is he the type to throw in the towel, but that first year was hard on him. That Ekaterinburg was a mere six hours by train from Verkhoturye probably saved us both. He came to visit often, once a month or so. I would look forward to these trips from the second I saw him get on the train to travel back to Verkhoturye.

Chris' train would always arrive in the evening. I worked until around eight and I'd head straight to the *vokzal.* I'd pace around the Soviet statues standing guard over the square in front of the station until Chris emerged.

"I drank four Baltika 9's on the train."

"Ok."

*

We didn't do much of anything. During the day, we'd wander aimlessly around the city. At night, we'd sit at my kitchen table with a bottle of Gzhelka, a cheap, but not too cheap, brand of vodka, and some beers, and munch on pistachios and *sukhariki* while listening to music.

We talked. A lot. These were not terribly deep conversations. We had made up a fake band in Training called the False Dmitris, and we'd go back and forth inventing ever more absurd stories about its imagined history and discography. We'd pose stupid questions about music we liked, and music we didn't like. We wrote endless top five lists, and devised elaborate toasts that preceded every drink. When one record came to an end, we'd take turns choosing which came next, prefacing each selection with a full discourse explaining and contextualizing our choice, as if we needed to justify putting on the Clash. Occasionally, we'd fall into a level of homesickness and wistfully pose questions about what we'd order if we were sitting at various restaurants in Chapel Hill we both liked. It was therapy for both of us. I'd go for days and days in Ekaterinburg without speaking to anyone beyond short, superficial interactions. With Chris, it was words flowing out like endless rain into a paper cup, like unleashing the cork on a bottle of Sovetskoe champagne.

It was nice just having someone to talk to.

If, on their face, our conversations were relatively shallow, they created a foundation for a lasting friendship. Chris and I still talk about these things. We have a shared vocabulary, a symbiosis, created through a continuous conversation and dialectic that now stretches over twenty years. We're still, at the base of our friendship, two lonely guys who needed each other to make it through a winter in the Urals.

*

Interlude: Let That Lonesome Whistle Chase My Blues
Away

There was a cage that you had to pass through to get into
my building in Ekaterinburg. I had to flash my ID and only
then would the *dezhurnaya* buzz it open. Chris and I
referred to the place as "Folsom."

*

My train leaves this minute
And it's a long ride to Dubuque
To be met at the station
By your kiss and rebuke

And I know it's not right
To go staring at the sun
But if I burn my eyes out
I'm not hurting anyone

Lord I would give everything I have
If I don't wake up sad
If I don't wake up
Lord I would give everything I have
If I don't wake up sad
If I don't wake up

The night's not worth nothing
If the train don't jump the track
And crash amongst the cornfields

And a couple smokestacks

'Cause I met a girl
I don't know where she's been
She's gonna wash away my sorrow
When she showers me with sin.

Lord I would give everything I have
If I don't wake up sad
If I don't wake up
Lord I would give everything I have
If I don't wake up sad
If I don't wake up

-        Ekaterinburg, 2002

Chris used to joke that all of my songs involved tea or trains, or drinking tea on trains. It's not an unfair observation. It's probably safe to say that ninety percent of my tea-drinking and train-riding was compressed into that period of my life. Tea was ritualized, and riding trains was a necessity. I didn't become a tea drinker, but I did fall in love with riding on trains. I would stare out the windows as the world slid by, as if I were stationary, and it was a panoramic picture that was being unscrolled before me. It was fascinating to watch the nothingness of Russia pass by, dotted by little towns here and there, or monuments to Socialism popping up in the distance, a Brutalist hammer and sickle rising from the earth in the middle of nowhere, or a Lenin statue perched on top of an anonymous hill.

I'm not sure why I chose Dubuque as the destination in this song. I don't have any connection to the town other than having driven through it a number of times, and it's not a word that flows or rhymes easily. That choice aside, I know for certain that I was imagining the Midwest in comparison to so much of the scenery I saw from train windows. I remember taking a bus from Vladimir to Suzdal with my parents when they visited me, and my dad commenting that the countryside reminded him of the farm he grew up on in Wisconsin. He was right of course. The interiors of the USA and Russia have a lot in common - vast areas of emptiness - «пустота» - the Russian word for "void" that seems so much more empty than "emptiness" possibly could - stretching in every direction to the horizon. The cornfields and smokestacks were as evocative of eastern Iowa as they were of Sverdlovskaya Oblast'.

Lyrically, I ripped off my friend Nate for the refrain. Sometime in the Fall of 2002, he sent me a CD with the songs he and his brother Matt had been recording that year back in Chapel Hill. One of them was called "Won't Wake Up Sad" and it really knocked me out. In it he sings, "I do everything I can so that you won't wake up sad." This seemed an impossibility. I woke every morning with a degree of sadness and loneliness, and there was no one around who could have fulfilled that promise. I certainly didn't think I could fulfill it for myself. What would I have to do to avoid waking up sad? I honestly had no idea. I deliberately repurposed this line and removed any hint of redemption. This is among the bleakest songs I wrote in Russia, along with "Rhode Island." "If I don't wake up" - self-nullification seemed to be the only way to avoid feeling

down. "If I burn my eyes out I'm not hurting anyone" -
again, reducing my own worth, as if I wasn't "anyone."

I was pretty sad at the time.

I wrote this as a slow tempo country song, pinching my
voice as I sang it. Later on, I began to play it faster, but I
was never satisfied with either version. I like the lyrics,
despite the tone. In graduate school I translated them into
Russian as a diversion from my studies. The song might
work better that way:

Поезд мой отправляет
И дольго до Дебюка
Меня подождешь на вокзале
С поцелуем и упреком

Я знаю не полезно
Смотреть на сольнце
Но если глаза загорятся
Только поранюсь сам

Боже, я бросил бы всё что у меня
Если не проснусь грустно
Если не проснусь
Ночь негодна
Если поезд сходит с рельсов
И врезается в поле рядом
С нескольким дымовым трубами

Но знакомился с девушкой
Не знаю как ее зовут
Она употреблит меня
И я забуду тебя

Боже, я бросил бы всё что у меня
Если не проснусь грустно
Если не проснусь

*

Interlude: Jesus, Help Me Find My Proper Place, or Jesus, Etc.

Most times when I passed the Catholic Church tucked away off the central square in Vladimir I thought about going in and lighting a candle. Later, in Ekaterinburg, I read the *Bhagavad Gita* and thought a lot about dharma. Russia is a good place to think about God because it's so easy to be sad there.

*

One of the reasons I was so sad in Ekaterinburg was that in so many ways I was unmoored. It wasn't just leaving Vladimir and feeling alone and isolated in a new city. Although much of the spring and summer of 2002 had been personally very joyful, international events made me feel really disillusioned. I didn't join the Peace Corps with a strong sense of idealism, but in the aftermath of September 11th, I thought that perhaps I had a role to play, living amongst the former "enemy," in making the world a better place. Moreover, as the US transitioned from aggrieved victim with the world's sympathy to vengeful leviathan thrashing about for retribution, I felt very strongly that my position out in the world could be a positive example to counter the caricature of the latest form of the Ugly American.

But as the march towards war in Iraq accelerated, I realized that this was foolish. No matter what I did, there was nothing I could do to compete with the actions of the Bush Administration. I could only watch from afar, helpless, as my country cynically manipulated people's grief and took actions that were so contrary to my ideals in order to pursue long-standing neo-imperialistic foreign policy goals. It was a loss of faith. Any idealism that I had - as a Peace Corps volunteer in the aftermath of September 11th, or just as a naive young person - evaporated. This was a heavy blow. I found myself in Ekaterinburg, alone, sad, missing my friends, and feeling disillusioned and disordered. Nothing made sense to me, nothing seemed hopeful. I started grasping at anything I could think of to give me some sort of grounding, to distract me from these feelings of helplessness.

Some of these attempts were unhealthy, physically and spiritually. I drank too much beer, and there was certainly an attempt to wash away my sorrows whenever Chris came to visit. If nothing else, the catharsis of a bottle of Gzhelka and some loud punk rock records felt good in the moment. But I also foolishly turned down offers from students and some folks at the Consulate to hang out. I'd offer up some lame excuse to beg off. It wasn't as if the people I met were cold or unwelcoming. They were as nice as anyone I had met in Vladimir, when I accepted just about every invitation extended to me. But by this point, I had retreated so far into a shell that it was really hard for me to snap out of the funk, and stasis seemed to be the only appropriate state of being.

Sometimes I managed to be a little more positive. On one of my trips into Moscow the previous year, I bought a copy of *The Brothers Karamazov*. I spent the winter and spring of 2002 wrestling my way through it. It had a pretty profound effect on me. I identified deeply with Dmitri, whose precarious position between his alternatively saintly and nihilistic brothers resonated a lot with me. He reminded me of Cody from *Desolation Angels*, which I also devoured at the time. Sometime in the fall of 2002, while leafing through *The Brothers Karamazov*, I zeroed in on one particular passage I had underlined, in which Dmitri is engaged in one of his regular crises of existence. After some tormented hand-wringing, he makes a resolution:

> There's no order in me, you see. And so everything is hell. My life has been one continual mess and disorder, but I'm going to try and put some order into it.

"I'm going to try and put some order into it."

My life seemed disordered too, and maybe by saying that out loud, and making a commitment to ordering it, I could snap out of the torpor I was in. It was what passed for a statement of purpose at the time, though my attempts to "put some order into it" were a little comical and misguided. I arrived at an admittedly convenient and unobtrusive spirituality that nonetheless seemed to offer solace, at least episodically. I became a vegetarian, even if I was an undisciplined one who incorporated lots of caveats and exceptions into my new lifestyle. I had the thought to get religion, so I bought and read a copy of the *Bhagavad Gita*. I started doing yoga and meditation. In my uninformed fumbling about how to actually practice these things, I stumbled upon a Buddhist tradition that suggested choosing your own mantra to focus the mind, so I chose a refrain that Dmitri quotes in *The Brothers Karamazov*, which in my translation was "Glory to the highest in the world, Glory to the highest in me." Before I knew it, I had constructed a spiritual practice which was remarkably similar to what I had read in *The Dharma Bums* and *Desolation Angels*, but if my attempts were rooted in bourgeois boho cliché, they helped me keep my sanity a bit.

*

I was never able to completely snap out of it, but happy moments came along from time to time. Sometimes I was up, like when several of my students organized a movie night for our class and invited me. We made lots of Russian salads with lots of mayonnaise and watched *Eyes Wide Shut*. It wasn't the film choice I was expecting, but it was a fun evening nonetheless.

My students were a bright spot of my time there. Like in Vladimir, they were only a few years younger than me. I taught night classes at the university. Anyone could sign up for them. There were a few people from the city, but most were university students, future managers and engineers on the Russian railroad system. My advanced class - the one that organized the movie night - was especially fun. I remember reading American literature with them - *The Raven* sticks out in my mind. I also remember having fun with a passage from an expat novel I had recently read called *12 Stories of Russia,* in which a Russian and an

American argue about whether Russian or English is a better language. It had a lot of good vocabulary - the American narrator makes a point of arguing that English is superior because its words have so many synonyms, after which he promptly lists a dozen variants of "walk" - and the students liked it because, while reading certain parts of it aloud, which they would invariably ask me to do, I would have to say Russian curse words, and colloquialisms like "халява," which they explained to me means "халява" when I asked about it. We always had a good laugh together. If I ever hit a stride teaching, it happened with that group.

And when class was over, I'd don my endless layers of winter clothes, and trudge out into the frigid night, walk along the windswept and frozen Iset, through the snow, back to my empty room. I'd unwrap myself and hang up my clothes, which I'd keep in a cabinet by the door.

*

Interlude: Perfect for Shattering

I remember arriving at a party thrown by one of the Consulate folks. As I was taking off my coat, I made an exclamation about the weather.

"Man, it's freezing outside."

"If it were freezing, it would be sixty degrees warmer than it is right now."

*

Hey she said the guy I'm with is such a bore
Do you wanna hang out well yeah I said sure
We walked down the boardwalk laughing and such
The planks 'neath our feet as our arms they did touch

The sun it was hotter than Havana in June
Oppressive like the Nazis as humid as a monsoon
And under the boardwalk our bodies lay wet
Sliding in rhythm all covered in sweat

She shoved off like the boats in the surf
And I took her wallet then for what it is worth
She went back to her sweetheart to try to put it to rest
And I stayed away at least I gave it my best

Still we stared at each other from fifty yards maybe more
Til I lost the contest and hit the liquor store

She steals away hey can you buy me a drink
Well this one's on me honey as towards me she did slink
And the night's not worth nothing if she don't keep track
'Cause I slashed her tires when she went out back

And it's not 'cause it's easy
And not 'cause I'm mean
When I know she is through with him
I guess I'll come clean

-      Ekaterinburg, 2002, maybe 2003

My memories of writing this was that I was deliberately trying to lay it on thick and be as absurd as possible. I like the line, "The sun it was hotter than Havana in June," and it goes downhill from there. I was imagining the boardwalk at Rehoboth Beach, Delaware, as well as the Jersey Shore, probably because I was listening to a lot of Bruce Springsteen at the time, and the summer heat was the inverse of the Ural winter that was frosting the inner pane of my double-paned windows. I don't think I ever played this for anyone - why would I? - but I do remember writing it, sitting at the table in my kitchen in Ekaterinburg. It was a fun evening.

*

Interlude: Train Round the Bend

I remember sitting in my apartment in Ekaterinburg and looking out on the city and seeing the trains at the station arriving and departing in the distance and wondering where they were going. I remember the dogs in the junkyard across the street waking me up in the morning with their incessant barking.

*

As Americans in Russia, we were enough of a curiosity to attract the attention of the local news media from time to time as subjects for human interest stories. These usually took the post-Cold War angle of "Russia and America - from enemies . . . to friends!" which was in stark contrast to the "Peace Corps Volunteers are engaging in espionage and working to destroy the country" stories that also ran every once in a while. I got pulled aside during our swearing-in ceremony in Moscow to mutter a few unintelligible words to the TV news covering the event, and the write up of our symposium on globalization passed for riveting news in Murom. The best example was when Simon was the subject of newspaper article about his life in Aginskoye, which detailed his supposed cultural metamorphosis, headlined to the effect of "The Day When 'Simon' Became *'Semyon.'*"

In December of 2002, a TV station in Ekaterinburg contacted me and asked if they could interview me about American holiday traditions for their morning show. They'd film it live from the ice castle that had been constructed in 1905 Square, beneath the colossal fir tree erected within the walls.

Sure.

On the appointed morning, they picked me up from my building in an SUV. I got in the backseat with the reporter, a woman about my age. As we headed downtown, she went over the choreography. We'd be joined by Ded Moroz and Snegurochka - Grandfather Frost and the Snow Maiden, his granddaughter who is traditionally cast as his "helper." The reporter was going to ask me about my impressions of Russia, a bit about Santa Claus, and what I was planning for New Year's, which in Russia is the centerpiece celebration of the season. She said Ded Moroz and Snegurochka might chime in with a question or two, but it wouldn't be anything unusual.

"Ok, you agree?" she asked.

"Yes, fine, good."

"No problems?"

"No problems."

The driver parked the SUV and we got out. The walls of the castle were enormous, about eight feet tall, made of blocks of ice. There were meticulously carved parapets and towers surrounding the perimeter of the square, which was about the size of a football field. A giant ice slide was carved into the keep. Kids lined up to climb to the top and slid at unsafe speeds down the slope, gliding across the ice until they were dumped onto the snow-covered asphalt. In the middle of the castle was a towering fir tree, decorated with lights. I could see Ded Moroz and Snegurochka waiting at its base.

The reporter introduced me and I shook hands with Ded Moroz, who was dressed in flowing blue robes, his fulsome white beard cascading down his chest, resting at the peak of his large belly. Snegurochka, despite the temperature being well below zero, was dressed in a short skirt, her tunic clinging to every curve on her body. She wore a blue hat that rested above her plucked eyebrows, the brim casting a shadow over her luxuriously long lashes. As I acknowledged Snegurochka, Ded Moroz made several suggestive grunts. Her eyelids fluttered open and closed and she giggled.

It was a weird beginning but I kept myself composed. The camera operator set up his equipment and the reporter asked if we were ready.

"Ready."

The camera operator counted off to action, and the reporter began speaking, introducing me to the audience. She asked me to tell the viewers about Santa Claus and American Christmas traditions. I was nervous, so I thought to keep it simple. I gave a short synopsis, delivering lines I had been practicing in my head. When I finished, I looked sheepishly at the camera, and awaited her next question.

So far, so good.

It was here that she went off script.

"Is it true Santa Claus likes to drink a lot?"

"Wait, what?"

"His nose is always red, yes?"

"I mean, I guess…"

"Do you think he drinks more than our Ded Moroz?"

"What?"

Ded Moroz let out a deep laugh.

"Ded Moroz likes to drink a lot!"

"Ded Moroz likes to drink a lot!" Ded Moroz repeated in the third person.

Ded Moroz laughed and Snegurochka giggled again.

"What?"

Ded Moroz smiled slyly.

"And what do you think of our Snegurochka?"

Snegurochka brushed her blonde locks over her shoulder and shifted her weight from one knee to the other, thrusting her hip towards me. She looked at me and winked.

"What?"

"What are you doing on New Year's? Maybe you could have a party with our Snegurochka!"

"But she's your granddaughter!"

All three of them laughed.

Some kids went down the ice slide, screaming and laughing. I glanced in their direction, but my eyes got distracted by Lenin, standing just beyond the walls of the ice castle. He was gesturing down the avenue, as if to say "This way to escape!"

From enemies to friends.

Save me Lenin.

"Do you agree that our Ded Moroz is better than your Santa Claus?"

"What?"

"I'm much prettier than Mrs. Claus! She's old!"

"What?"

I kept waiting for some indication that I had been duped into participating in a prank show of some sort, a Russian version of Ali G or whatever, but it never happened. I left the last question unanswered, an awkward silence creating dead air. The reporter jumped in to wrap up the proceedings. She asked all of us to wish the audience at home a Happy New Year. I gave a shell-shocked wish of holiday cheer, more "S Novym *god damn*" than "*S Novym godom.*"

We got back in the SUV and drove silently back across the city.

"Thank you *Dooglas,* that was great. *S Novym godom!*"

God damn.

She offered me her hand.

From friends to enemies.

God damn.

*

Interlude: London Calling

I listened to the BBC World News every night during the week and felt sad and isolated when it went off the air at ten o'clock. The cricket scores made no sense.

*

New Jersey misses you
The same goes for me
'Cause I've been sleeping alone here
Since you left the country

And I know it's not right
To go staring at the sun
But it's the only thing I can see
That's farther away from me
Than where you've gone

New Jersey misses you
The same goes for me
I'd light a candle for you
But you're not lost at sea

So this one's for whiskey
And this one's for regret
And this one's for the party
That's been a drag ever since you left

-        Ekaterinburg, 2002, maybe 2003

So many of the songs I wrote in Russia have a geography.
Rhode Island. Maine. Dubuque. New Jersey. Even Paris
and Madrid. Much of this is songwriting trope. The art
form has always been imbued with geography, real or
imagined, and I certainly fell back on this a lot. It's not a
coincidence that there are no mentions of Russian cities in

any of my songs. Of course, there is the obvious fact that the linguistic differences between Russian and English make it unlikely that a Russian city name would flow or sound good. More likely it is that I was using the tried and true device of fantasizing about being somewhere else. So much American songwriting is aspirational after all, about writing an escape from your present condition. The trains I mentally hopped were the lyrical descendants of following Highway 61 out of town.

The songs I wrote in Ekaterinburg in particular have this sense of displacement. This was true for a couple of reasons I suppose. One was that from my kitchen window you could see across the city to the railway station. I could see the trains arriving and departing at all hours, but they were especially vivid at night. There's a novella by Viktor Pelevin set on a train called *The Yellow Arrow* that I had read several years before, and that's what those trains looked like to me, yellow arrows, their glowing windows streaking across the horizon. I used to imagine the stories of people on those trains, some heading east towards Siberia, some heading west, across the Urals to Europe.

The other reason I liked watching those trains was for no other reason than imagining myself in a place that was likely happier than where I was. I knew I was lonely and sad in Ekaterinburg; it was easy to imagine things being better in Maine, in Rhode Island, in Dubuque even. There was a novel that was popular at the time called *Prague*. I never read it but apparently it was about a bunch of American expatriates in Budapest fantasizing about being in Prague, a Shangri-La that was unattainable to them. This was very resonant with me. I couldn't focus on where I was since I was so alone and still in shock about having been forced to move there and I was determined to wallow in that pity. The books I read and the records I listened to encouraged this sense of displacement. I reread *On the Road* during this time, Sal Paradise's jaunts serving not as a roadmap for my adolescent fantasies this time, but as an aspiration to go somewhere else, physically or metaphysically, it didn't matter.

I sought to capture the bleakness I was feeling in this song, although I redirected its source as someone having left me, rather than me leaving everything that was comforting and familiar. There was a self-destructiveness to it, embodied by the line, "I know it's not right to go staring at the sun," a line I used in two songs I wrote in Ekaterinburg. I remember the second half of that line, "but it's the only thing I can see that's farther away from me than where you've gone," coming to me as I walked around town soon after I arrived. It was a sunny day, one the few while I was there, and I guess my eyes were drawn to it. I even remember that I thought of it as I walked past a statue of Pushkin near where I lived, though this was just coincidence. It's not a line Pushkin would've written, and there's certainly no connection between it popping into my head and that statue. It's just an image lodged in my mind.

I've come to like this song a lot though I didn't think much of it when I wrote it. I thought it needed a refrain, but I like its simplicity.

Interlude: I Heart NY, or 9/11 Changed Everything

I hung a New York for the Olympics poster on the wall over my bed in Ekaterinburg and believed it.

*

Since she went back to Maine
I just haven't been the same
I've been making the rounds
Of all the sin that can be found
From the Bronx to Brooklyntown

And when she gave me back that ring
I went and pawned the goddam thing
I bought a ticket underground
And I rode that railway all around
From the Bronx to Brooklyntown

-        Ekaterinburg, 2002

I remember writing this at the kitchen table in my apartment in Ekaterinburg. By this point, I was starting, far too late, to think about life after Peace Corps. Adam had moved to New York after he got kicked out of Russia, and I was considering following him there. He had written the phrase "back to Brooklyn" in an email to me and I used that as a starting point, scribbling ideas in between classes one night in December 2002 before polishing them up at home.

I wasn't broken-hearted, but I was very lonely, and sought to, again, document this feeling. One of my favorite songs at the time was Nina Simone's "Break Down and Let It All Out," and I embraced that sentiment wholeheartedly, putting pen to paper over and over and over again as an attempt, however unsuccessful, to put it to rest, to maybe get some release, because "holding back ain't gonna do no good."

The aimless riding around on the subway was taken from my practice of passing days in Ekaterinburg the same way. I also had in my mind the Belle and Sebastian lyric, "Riding on city busses for a hobby is sad."

It is.

This was also one of the first songs in which I considered the idea of marriage as a real possibility, rather than something that people older than me did. Several of my friends got married while I was in Russia. It seemed as if a passage into adulthood was happening for my peers while I was ensconced in a far corner of the earth, avoiding any manner of reality and responsibility. But some rubicon had been crossed, and this life transition percolated down, even to me. It was in Russia that I started to look at women's hands when I first met them to see if there was a ring on their finger. When I got back home, I continued this practice, although I had to culturally recalibrate and switch from looking at her right hand to her left.

I did some fact-checking for this song, asking Adam if it was possible to ride from the Bronx to Brooklyn entirely underground before I committed to the lyric.

This is the only song I wrote in Russia that had a bit of an afterlife. A year later, I added a chorus and recorded it with Matt and Nate. But it will always be a Russia song.

***

Through the Changing Ocean Tides

After the tumult of the summer, Peace Corps' position vis-a-vis the Russian government seemed to stabilize. Kicking out half of our group, and preventing a new cohort from arriving that August, had served as close enough to a pound of flesh to satisfy our antagonists. I wasn't under any illusions that Peace Corps had a future in Russia, but it appeared fairly likely that we would be able to finish our terms and depart the following summer.

With that timeline in mind, Chris and I started to discuss the possibility of him moving sites to Ekaterinburg. He was as unhappy in Verkhoturye as I was in Ekaterinburg. We had gotten pretty good at being miserable together in spurts; why not try it on a long-term basis? Apart from that, his teaching situation had deteriorated. In November, he wrote to me "there is no need, or desire, for me or any other PCV to be here . . . and I never should have been sent here in the first place." It was a long shot, but I went so far as to have preliminary discussions with Elena Ivanovna about whether he could get a job at my university. Perhaps it was a way that both of us could finish the last leg of our service on a positive note.

We also began to plan our grand finale. During one of his visits, Chris and I sat at my kitchen table and sketched out an ambitious trek into Siberia for the coming year. We decided to go to Baikal again - Chris had worked at the same camp as I did during a different session - before riding the Trans-Siberian to its terminus at Vladivostok and making our way back west via China and Mongolia - a 10,000-mile-long capstone to our service. It was something to look forward to.

*

That Peace Corps' time in Russia was in its endgame was pretty well confirmed when the Moscow office organized a conference in December for the remaining Volunteers. It had been the norm for us to all descend on the capital from time to time, but all of these gatherings had an ostensible practical purpose - the previous March, after we had been at site for six months; that summer, to get our visas renewed. This one seemed pretty superfluous, as if the office knew it was over and decided to spend the money it had in the bank because otherwise it would go unused.

It was great. For a few days we got to live off the Program's relative largesse. There were a couple of perfunctory workshops, but mostly it was just social, an opportunity for us to spend time together, to get a mental break, to feel connected after a period when so many of our connections had been severed. The office staff arranged for us to have a belated Thanksgiving dinner at the US Embassy dacha at Serebryany Bor. Somehow, Melanie and Chris and Simon and Andrew and Rob and I managed to talk our way into spending the night there the night before the party. We had to cook the meal, but it was an easy thing to volunteer for. We drank beer, watched a VHS tape of episodes of *The Simpsons* my friend Brandon had sent me, and managed not to incinerate the turkey despite our best attempts.

When the weekend was over, I flew back to Ekaterinburg. That same day, Nikolai Patrushev, the Director of the FSB, gave an interview to state television in which he stated that the reason that so many Volunteers had been denied visas earlier in the year was because, "Some of them were engaged in collecting information about the sociopolitical and economic situation in Russian regions, about government employees and administrators, and the course of elections."

Essentially, he accused us of espionage.

I don't have any idea whether the timing of this interview had anything to do with us being in Moscow or not. Probably it was just a coincidence, but it had an eeriness to it, as if they wanted to let us know that they were watching us, for the FSB is not an organization that typically operates in a coincidental world. At the very least, this was the first public indication of how certain high-level sectors of the Russian government viewed the Peace Corps, or at least how they wanted to tar us. Later on, several other officials gave interviews suggesting that the friction between the Peace Corps and the Russian government was due to our lack of qualifications for the positions we held, which, to be fair, wasn't entirely ridiculous. But calling us spies was sinister.

When I landed in Ekaterinburg, I climbed into a *marshrutka* to take me into the city. I was sitting in the back, crammed in with six other people, when Patrushev's remarks were reported on the radio station we were listening to. I felt a pit in my stomach and looked around at my fellow passengers.

Some of them were dozing off.

Some of them were staring blankly out of the window.

"Some of them were engaged in collecting information about the sociopolitical and economic situation in Russian regions, about government employees and administrators, and the course of elections."

*

I was spooked. I wrote to my friend Nate a few days later, "Though of course no one in the van knew who I was, I did feel like I was in one of those movies where, like, a wanted poster gets put up and all the people realize it's the dude standing in the same line at the bank." I started carrying my passport with me around town instead of my Peace Corps ID in case I got stopped by the *Militsiya*.

On December 16th, the day after I got home to Ekaterinburg, *The Moscow Times*, an English-language newspaper, published an article detailing Patrushev's comments, which I forwarded to my family and friends, accompanied by a postscript: "[T]o those KGB spooks who are reading this email, do one of the following: leave us alone or kick us out of here. I'm sick of this."

However, as dire as things seemed, it was also a bit of the same old story. True, Patrushev himself going on record was a big deal. It was also rather ominous that he seemed to lump us in the same category as a "Turkish extremist sect" engaged in "pan-Turkic and pan-Islamic brainwashing of Russian teenagers" in the interview. But if this was an escalation of rhetoric, it didn't radically alter my view of our position. After detailing my reaction to the radio report in the *marshrutka* to Nate, I ended the email by writing, "It'd be cool if you could come hang out." The story was pretty simple from my point of view - they don't like us, but they'll be done with us next August. And maybe Nate could come visit in the meantime.

If my assessment of our situation was what passed for optimism, it was misplaced. On Christmas Day, as I sat at my kitchen table, playing Solitaire and listening to Nick Drake, before I caught the subway downtown to finally liberate the expensive copy of *Mingus Ah Um* from the glass case in which it was ensconced in an electronics store near the Afghanistan memorial, the Russian government withdrew from the agreement that allowed Peace Corps to operate in the country.

It was too much to let us finish our service and walk away.

We had ninety days to get out.

*

One of the first times I ever walked on Red Square, in March of 1991, it was snowing. A group of us from the school trip I was on took the Metro downtown from our hotel in Ostankino to pay homage to the first Pizza Hut in the Soviet Union. We ate greasy pizza and drank Pepsi, the placemats on the tables adorned with Soviet and American flags. Afterwards, we took the leftovers and walked across Red Square, snowflakes the size of quarters falling on our heads, before tumbling onto the bricks of the square. We posed for a picture in front of St. Basil's Cathedral, holding the pizza box prominently in front of us. Earlier that day, just yards away, I had climbed onto the shoulders of a friend of mine to take pictures of the changing of the guard at Lenin's Mausoleum, the goose-stepping soldiers locked in choreographed precision, their movements as sharp as the bayonets fixed to their Kalashnikovs. It was an odd juxtaposition to be sure, but indicative of the times - the end of the Cold War, the dawn of a new age. It seemed as likely as anything for those soldiers to keep goose-stepping down to Pizza Hut for a personal pan pizza once their watch was over.

The next year, Russia would welcome its first group of Peace Corps Volunteers.

From enemies to friends.

Nearly twelve years later, on January 5, 2003, I again found myself wandering around Red Square in the snow. This time I was alone. I was supposed to have met up with an old friend from St. Petersburg, but he'd missed his train, and so it was just me, standing before the towering walls of the Kremlin, by the red granite step pyramid in which the communists had entombed Lenin, strolling around the windswept square. The footsteps I could hear were not those of the polished boots of the honor guard clacking on the pavement at Lenin's Mausoleum, but of my own scuffed Doc Martens muffled by the wet snow.

"Bummed around Red Square this morning. Snowing and beautiful," I wrote to my parents later that day.

"With the thought of leaving Russia soon, it feels different."

About a half mile away, in the Lubyanka, was Nikolai Patrushev's office.

"It feels different."

From friends to enemies.

God damn.

*

I was in Moscow to meet Melanie. Our universities were both on an extended winter break, and rather than sit idly in Uglich and Ekaterinburg, we decided to go traveling while we still could. The timing of our inevitable departure from Russia was still unclear at this point, but we knew it was coming soon. Within a short period of time, we'd have to go back to America. For all the frustration and stress and angst and sadness I had felt over the past few months, going back home - back to reality - was scary. I knew a chapter in my life that was unlikely to be approximated ever again was coming to a close.

We spent a couple of days in Moscow before boarding a train to Tallinn. We had vague plans about spending some time in Estonia, and maybe Finland, before going to Uglich. The trip was pretty low energy. It was cold and dark, and I was pretty frazzled about everything. We had fun, and Tallinn, decked out in holiday lights and covered in snow, was beautiful. But it was hard to ignore the rest of the noise.

A few days after we arrived in Tallinn, Peace Corps called us at our hostel to tell us that it was over. The Program was closing. We had to leave Russian territory by February 15th. It was kind of funny getting this message while in Estonia. We'd have to travel back to Russia just to get expelled from it.

The Irony of Fate.

*

The next day, Melanie and I returned to Russia. The border guards barely batted an eyelash at our documents when we hit Russian customs late at night. If there was any sort of APB out on Peace Corps Volunteers on the loose, it hadn't made it to this particular checkpoint. Whatever threat we may have posed wasn't acute enough to prevent our coming back.

We went up to Uglich for a few days, but we didn't do much. I remember walking out onto the frozen surface of the Volga, and checking out a cathedral that was built to commemorate the spot where Ivan the Terrible's son Dmitri may or may not have been murdered. But that was it. There wasn't much to the town, and my mood for exploration was minimal in any event.

It was nice being back together with Melanie again, even if everything was tempered with exhaustion. We started talking about the future. About the final Close of Service Conference which was scheduled to start on February 7th, just a few weeks away. We talked about traveling home. About possibly meeting up in London on the way. About getting the group - the two of us and Adam and Laura and Simon and Chris and Rob and Andrew - together back in the States somehow. About moving to Chicago when all was said and done. There was a lot of uncertainty, some of which was exciting, some of which was scary, and sad. We only knew one thing for sure.

Peace Corps was ending.

It was time to sail through the changing ocean tides.

I got back to Ekaterinburg on January 18th. I had three weeks until I had to be back in Moscow, and I didn't have much to do during this time. I brooded a bit about what had happened to Peace Corps, but I was also liberated from the sadness I had been feeling for so long. I spent my days taking in Ekaterinburg while I could, walking around the city. It was pretty, constantly blanketed with snow. I stood on the frozen city pond near where I lived and watched a crane hoist the gold cupolas onto the pillars of the Church on Blood in Honor of All Saints Resplendent in the Russian Land that was under construction. I took valedictory walks down Prospekt Lenina and stopped for one last bowl of plov at the Uzbek restaurant Chris and I had discovered. I wasn't afforded this kind of goodbye when I left Vladimir. For all the sadness I experienced in Ekaterinburg, I did feel an affection for the city, and I was glad that I could walk its avenues one final time.

Chris came for one last visit. We spent a lot of time playing records by the Clash - Joe Strummer had died only a few weeks before - and talking about our trek home. Chris had ambitious plans to get lost in Europe for a while, and I was tempted to join him, but in the end, we went in different directions. In the long run though, I didn't have any worries about seeing Chris again after Peace Corps. I somehow knew our orbits around each other were set.

One day, Chris and I went with a colleague from the university to a ski slope in the Urals just west of Ekaterinburg, on the other side of the imaginary line that divides Europe from Asia. On our way back to the city, we stopped at the plaza alongside the highway marking the continental divide. As there is along the train tracks, there's an obelisk, as well as a ceremonial line of bricks dividing the plaza - and Eurasia - in two. It was snowing - of course it was - but someone had swept the line clean. Chris and I posed for a picture, standing on either side of the demarcation, him in Asia, me in Europe.

It was fitting. Chris and I can be on two different continents, but we'll always be close together.

*

A few weeks later, Chris was back in town. We were joined by Andrew and Rob and Simon, who stopped into Ekaterinburg on their way to Moscow from Krasnoyarsk. We'd all travel together to the Close of Service Conference that was about to begin.

I had spent the previous couple of days tying up loose ends - closing my bank account, returning materials I had borrowed from the university. It was like switching off a machine through a series of prescribed steps, this switch turned before that one. I was powering down my life in Russia. In what seemed particularly symbolic of my impending departure, I took my parka to the Voznesensky Cathedral, a pretty eighteenth century baroque cathedral in the city, and donated it to charity. The garment that had insulated me from so much that Russia threw at me, that I had purchased via the efforts of Ludmilla Anatolovna at the *rynok* in Vladimir, was about to become superfluous, like a second skin or exoskeleton I was shedding because it was no longer needed. There's winter in America of course, but it's not the same.

It feels different.

I stressed about what to do with my guitar. I couldn't take it with me, however much I wanted to. Chris and I made jokes about taking it outside and smashing it on the icy sidewalk, but that didn't seem right. I've read several interviews with musicians who discuss instruments as mere tools, that one guitar is like the next is like the next. Perhaps I'm too sentimental, but that never made much sense to me. My guitar was like a friend. It had been a constant companion through my time in Russia, and I felt as if I was abandoning a comrade. It pained me to leave it behind. Destroying it was out of the question. When it was time to leave, I strummed one last chord - D minor, the saddest of keys - and set it in the corner of my room, letting the vibrations reverberate until the tones faded into silence.

At least I still had the composition book in which I had written all my songs. I'd keep that forever.

The Irony of Fate.

The only bit of unfinished business was the bottle of vodka Adam had given me when left. I was waiting for a suitable occasion to drink it, and this seemed to be it. Chris, Simon, Rob, Andrew and I crowded around my tiny kitchen table. Since I didn't have enough glasses for everybody, we decided to pour our shots into plastic measuring cups. It was a final example of that combination of Peace Corps ingenuity and Peace Corps alcoholism.

We gave toasts, but they were pretty simple. It was time to get on with it, no sense in delay.

As we raised our measuring cups, I made sure to give a little nod towards New York, towards Adam, then I downed it.

It was awful.

*

Interlude: It's Good to Be on the Road Back Home Again

I remember Chris, Rob, Simon, Andrew, and I walking one
by one across a frozen pond on the way to the *vokzal* to
catch our train to Moscow. My luggage was so heavy I was
worried the ice would break.

*

The night before we went out to site in October 2001, the
Ambassador hosted us at Spaso House, a neoclassical
mansion that served as his official residence in Moscow.
Its grand interior has witnessed a lot of fantastical intrigue
over the years. William Bullitt, the first American
ambassador to the Soviet Union, was known for the
extravagant parties he hosted at Spaso House, which
sometimes involved trained seals and bears, one of which
was got inebriated after being served champagne by Karl
Radek, a Bolshevik revolutionary who was later murdered
in a Stalinist labor camp. One of these soirées inspired
Mikhail Bulgakov, who reimagined the 1935 Spring
Festival as Satan's Ball in *The Master and Margarita*. During
the ball, Margarita is led to the top of a grand staircase that
was so high that from the top, the foyer below looked so
small that "she may have been looking through the wrong
end of an opera glass." Margarita is tasked with greeting a
parade of dead souls summoned from the underworld to
Satan's Ball, entering this astral plane through the fireplace
at the base of the staircase. She stands there for hours,
becoming more and more uncomfortable and exhausted,

until at last, she "quivered with joy: the stream of guests was thinning."

Our reception there wasn't quite as fantastical. The Ambassador and the Peace Corps Country Director gave some remarks, Anya and I delivered a speech in Russian, after which we were sworn in.

The next day, I went to Vladimir.

*

In February 2003, we didn't have an oath to take. Upon our arrival in Moscow, instead of raising our right hands, we reached into our pockets and surrendered our Peace Corps IDs to Larissa, an employee of the Moscow office. She scrawled «НЕДЕЙСТВИТЕЛЬНО» - "void" - in green marker on them, and returned them to us. Only Chris refused to hand his over. Deciding to go out on his own terms, he removed his card from his pocket, ripped it in half, and threw it in the trash. We were no longer Peace Corps Volunteers, not quite Returned Peace Corps Volunteers. We were voided.

НЕДЕЙСТВИТЕЛЬНО.

We spent several days going through the closing bureaucracy, writing reports, taking language tests, having discussions about what we'd done, what we might do now. The Director of the Peace Corps, Gaddi Vasquez, showed up to officially close the program. At one of the luncheons, I found myself sitting next to him. The only topic of conversation that seemed to excite him was his newly acquired George Foreman Grill, about which he expounded at length. This didn't bother me; I wasn't in the mood for any high-minded conversations anyway.

Interspersed with everything were valedictory jaunts around Moscow - final strolls across Red Square, or down Tverskoi Bulvar, a trip to the souvenir market at Ismailovo. Perhaps as another way to use the remaining funds in the accounts, Peace Corps put us up at the Hotel Ukraina, a Stalinist skyscraper on the Moskva River. We had a cluster of rooms on the nineteenth floor. We referred to one of them, #1905, as "The Revolution Room." They had high ceilings and deep red carpet. The door knobs were brass.

The remaining Volunteers from the Far East joined us in Moscow. They were as decimated as us. Our groups didn't interact much. They had their own program to close, their own comrades to enjoy in the waning days of this extraordinary period of their lives. We'd see them in the lobby, milling about. It had to be strange for them. They had never been to Moscow. We at least had the comfort of our surroundings to ground us in such a weird time. Everything was alien to them.

My immediate future was as ill-defined as ever. I went to the Aeroflot ticketing office on Novy Arbat and bought a flight to Oslo, where an old friend from St. Petersburg lived. I thought I'd go visit him and figure everything else out from there. I had a ticket home from London in early March. In the meantime, I could go just about anywhere.

I just couldn't stay in Russia.

*

We returned to Spaso House on our last night in Russia.

The Ambassador was hosting a farewell party for us. The staff from the Moscow office were all there, as well as some other guests. Boris has flown in from Ekaterinburg for the closing ceremony.

We arrived after a short ride over from the Hotel Ukraina, and were led into the Chandelier Room. The room was massive and grand, with Ionic columns and barrel vaults, the walls decked out with Modern Art. A massive crystal chandelier hung from the ceiling. Off to the side was a table, with white tablecloths and a couple of bartenders. The table was covered in bottles of Budweiser.

I spent the evening in a manic rush, bouncing around the room, hearing stories from Ivan about his time crushing the Prague Spring on his *beeez-neees treep* with the Soviet Army, and getting a lesson in Charles Mingus' discography from the Ambassador, receiving photographs with wry comments about Marxism-Leninism from Elena. And taking pictures with everybody - *Dooglas, give me your camera* - so many people who had had such an impact on my life, most of whom I would never see again.

Как здорово, что все мы здесь.
Сегодня собрались.

At the end of the evening, we were corralled onto the grand staircase off the chandelier room that had inspired Bulgakov. We arranged ourselves on the steps, a graduated portrait of what remained of our cohort, fifty-six whittled down to nineteen. We had posed on the same spot sixteen months before, after we were sworn in. In that picture, Adam is standing in front of me. Texas Mike peeks out from the mass of faces filling up the staircase. Laura poses in between Melanie and Simon. It was so crowded you can't even make out Chris or Rob or Andrew. This time, there wasn't such a problem. Our group only stretched halfway up the staircase.

The stream of guests had thinned.

*

When we returned to the hotel, I found myself on the front steps, standing with Boris in the frigid night air. After a few silent moments, Boris and I shook hands, and said our goodbyes. He retreated into the hotel, and I was left alone. I didn't linger very long - the party was set to continue upstairs. But I took a few minutes to get one last look of Moscow at night.

It was beautiful, the cold blackness of the winter night speckled with all the lights of the city, the chill in the air somehow putting everything in sharper contrast. Cars whooshed down Kutuzovsky Prospekt, their blurred headlights like shooting stars streaking down the boulevard. The White House, illuminated by floodlights, stood on the opposite bank of the Moskva River. In the distance, the Ministry of Foreign Affairs towered over the Arbat. Like the Hotel Ukraina, it is one of the Seven Sisters, the Stalinist skyscrapers that dominate Moscow's skyline. One of their siblings, the Leningradskaya Hotel, stood on the other side of the city, on Komsomolskaya Square. From any of the three *vokzals* that share the square, I could catch a train just to just about anywhere in Russia. To St. Petersburg. To Vladimir. To Murom and Nizhny Novgorod. To Ekaterinburg. To Irkutsk and beyond.

I could do it, visa issues be damned. I could go up to my room, grab my shoulder bag, and go.

But of course I didn't.

On the nineteenth floor, my bags were packed. Inside was the *telnyashka* from Tamara, and a rock from Baikal my secret friend had given me, and a small palekh box Ludmilla Anatolovna gave me when I left Vladimir.

In my shoulder bag was my copy of *Desolation Angels* which I had started rereading, even though I already knew how it ended:

> A peaceful sorrow at home is the best I'll ever be able to offer the world, in the end, and so I told my Desolation Angels goodbye. A new life for me.

*

Postlude: I got a home on high, in another land, so far away

The next morning, as I sat in Sheremetyevo waiting for my flight to leave, I wrote out a list of grievances and frustrations about Russia - that I was being kicked out, that I had been expelled from Vladimir, that Aeroflot had just charged me a hundred dollars in overweight baggage fees, that the currency exchange counter where I needed to change my dollars into rubles so I could pay the fine was closed for lunch at eight o'clock in the morning.

I scribbled the list furiously, then paused, before adding, "And all of this *is* Russia's fault, but you know you love it anyway."

Then I got on a plane and flew to Oslo.

Поехали.

***

*

Glossary of Russian Terms

Babushka (бабушка) - Everyone knows this word. It means "grandmother" but generally has the meaning of a tough, industrious older woman. In Russian, the stress is placed on the first syllable.

Baltika (Балтика) - The most popular brand of Russian beer. Ubiquitous. The varieties were numbered, 0 to 9. Baltika 3, referred to colloquially as "troika," was by far the most popular. It was a tasteless, inoffensive macrobrew lager. Baltika 7 tasted exactly the same but was for some reason referred to as "Export." Baltika 9 was called "Extra Lager." It was high alcohol. There were rumors that it was brewed with vodka, but that always struck me as an absurd myth to explain its ungodly flavor.

Banya - A Russian bathhouse. You sit in a hot room, sweat, drink beer, and occasionally beat each other with birch branches. It's heavenly.

Bogatyr (богатырь) - A legendary knight of Russian myth, akin to a Knight of the Round Table.

Dezhurnaya (дежурная) - A woman (it's always a woman) stationed at the entrance to a dormitory or, in Soviet times, on each floor of a hotel, who controlled who could and who couldn't enter.

Durak (дурак) - Durak is the best card game ever invented.

Gopnik (гопник) – A term used for a young working-class Russian. The stereotype is that they are always wearing Adidas tracksuits and drinking cheap beer and spitting sunflower seeds all over the place.

Халява (khalyava) - Халява means халява.

Khrushchyovka (Хрущёвка) - A portmanteau of *Khrushchev* and *trushchoba,* the Russian word for "slum." This is a term given to the mass produced five-story apartment blocks that were built all over the Soviet Union during the Khrushchev era. What started out as a dig has evolved into a term of endearment.

Lubyanka - The Lubyanka is the headquarters of the FSB in Moscow. It also served in the same capacity for the various Soviet security services. There was an old Soviet joke about it being the tallest building in Moscow because you could see Siberia from its basement.

Marshrutka (маршрутка) - Minibus taxis that run somewhat regular, somewhat irregular routes. Marshrutki typically mirror established bus routes, but don't always stop at all the stops. If you want to get in, you hail it like a taxi. If you want to get out, you call out to the driver to stop at the next stop. There really isn't any sort of maximum capacity; capacity is however many people can cram in the back. Once inside, you pay your fare by passing the money to the person next to you that is closer to the driver that you are. That person passes it forward and so on until it makes it to the driver. If change is required, the process repeats itself in reverse. Marshrutki drivers' observance of local traffic laws is sometimes minimal. There's a marshrutka driver video game that I've played that deducts points if you ram into the Militsiya but *not* if you run over pedestrians. It's pretty true to life.

Militsiya (Милиция) - The police.

Некультурный (nyekulturnii) - Literally "uncultured" although it has a connotation that suggests the person being labeled "некультурный" is uneducated or uncouth or of a lower stratum of existence. It can be a pretty pointed rebuke to lob at someone.

Oblast' (область) - Region/province.

Obschezhitiye (общежитие) - Dormitory.

ОВИР (OVIR) - The Department for Visas and Registration. By law, as a foreigner you had to register your passport and visa at the ОВИР if you were planning to stay in a city for more than three days.

Podmoskovye - Region around Moscow.

Поехали (poyekhali) - "Let's go."

Produkty (Продукты) - A grocery store. Some of these were like little supermarkets, but many are tiny little corner groceries, with separate counters for meat, produce, bread and the like. You would have to ask for everything you wanted individually - a loaf of bread, or a link of sausage, or four Baltikas, or whatever. A shopping bag cost an extra ruble.

Rasputitsa (распутица) - The period in both spring and fall, during which rain, and melting snow, turns much of Russia into a muddy quagmire. The rasputitsa has been credited, in part, with such impressive feats as defeating both Napoleon and the Fascists, but mostly it just makes a mess of everything.

Rynok (рынок) - Market or bazaar, frequently open air, but not always. Any town of any size had a rynok and you could find just about anything there.

S Novym godom (С Новым годом) - Happy New Year!

Samogon (самогон) - Moonshine.

Sukhariki (сухарики) - Ribbon-like croutons that were a common accompaniment for beer.

Telnyashka (Тельняшка) - a ubiquitous striped undershirt that has origin in the Russian and Soviet armed forces. A lot of times they are tank tops, but they can also be long-sleeved. I was told that it is некультурный to wear one in public.

Troika (тройка) – A traditional Russian sled pulled by three horses. "Troika" is also shorthand for Baltika 3, the most popular Russian beer. Asking for a troika is similar to saying "Gimme a Bud."

Varenye (варенье) - Fruit preserves, frequently made from berries.

Владимировец (Vladimirovets) - A person from Vladimir.

Vokzal (вокзал) - Train station.

Yorsh (ёрш) - A mixture of beer and vodka.

***

*

Bibliography

Akhmatova, A., Kunitz, S., & Hayward, M. (1997). *Poems of Akhmatova* (1st THUS ed.). Mariner Books.

Bulgakov, M. A., & Ginsburg, M. (1994). *The Master and Margarita.* Chico, CA: Avalon Travel Publishing.

Dostoevsky, F., MacAndrew, A. R., & Mochulsky, K. (1984). *The Brothers Karamazov* (Bantam Classics) (Reissue ed.). Bantam Classics.

Herr, M. (1991). *Dispatches* (Reprint ed.). Vintage.

Kerouac, J. (1995). *Desolation Angels.* New York, NY: Riverhead Books.

Kerouac, J., & Charters, A. (1991). *On the Road* (Penguin Twentieth Century Classics) (Revised ed.). Penguin Classics.

Rasputin, V., Mikkelson, G., & Winchell, M. (1997). *Siberia, Siberia* (Translated ed.). Northwestern University Press.

***